PRAISE FOR *THE F*
BUSINESS

'This book made me re-evaluate our internal communications entirely, and its importance at the centre of a global business. I run a successful "people business" and this book has reminded me, simply and clearly, that I can be doing so much more to communicate internally to ensure inspiration, motivation and loyalty among our most important company asset – our talent.' **Molly Aldridge, Global CEO, M&C Saatchi PR**

'*The People Business* is a fantastic testament to how internal communication has found its professional feet and is driving organizational performance with a unique and valuable set of skills, knowledge and expertise. At the Institute of Internal Communication (IoIC) we are committed to raising the profile and credibility of the profession and are delighted to support this book with its contribution from the IoIC President, Suzanne Peck.' **Jennifer Sproul, Chief Executive, Institute of Internal Communication**

'A rare and practical guide for what good IC looks like from people that actually do it.' **Gavin Ellwood, Founder and Director, Ellwood Atfield**

'Running a business has never been more complicated. Being able to deal with fast-changing external risk demands a clear understanding of your internal audience. That's part of what Q&R do; and that understanding is what Annabel Dunstan and Imogen Osborne have shared in this timely and vital book.' **Ian Henderson, CEO of communications agency AML Group**

'A clear, simple, easy-to-read, case-study-led book for anyone who wants to unlock the secrets of internal communications and employee engagement. I believe that real-life examples always give the deepest insights; this is great content for practitioners, experts and novices alike.' **BJ Cunningham, speaker, brand guru and renowned entrepreneur**

'You can't take people with you unless they know what's going on and feel involved. Not in a fast-paced, multichannel world. In *The People Business* internal communications experts bare all in the name of best practice.' **Tanya Hughes, President, SERMO Communications, Talk PR**

'Dunstan and Osborne have assembled an outstanding group of people at the leading edge of thinking and practice in engagement communications. Page after page of provocative ideas and practical insight make *The People Business* a landmark book in the development of the craft of workplace communications. The authors embrace the reality that internal communications is at an inflection point in its development. Leaders know that they want good communications and that traditional tools are not effective any more. Dunstan and Osborne explore with their interviewees crucial current issues such as the role of date, audience understanding and what employee engagement really means.' **Liam FitzPatrick, Managing Partner, Working Communication, and co-author of *Internal Communications*, also published by Kogan Page**

'A book that gives a real feel for the issues confronting internal communications teams – remote working, multichannel media, millennial expectations – and shows how 10 top firms are trying to tackle them. Each chapter can be used to stimulate classroom discussion and learning about real business challenges.' **Trevor Morris, Professor of Public Relations, Richmond University, and Former Chairman/CEO of several companies in the PR and recruitment industries**

'*The People Business* is a fascinating look into the world of internal communications, acknowledging its humble beginnings while looking ahead to its continuing evolution as a critical business function. It tells the stories of 10 companies that are getting IC right and takes a realistic look at the challenges facing IC practitioners today. From managing change to the impact of millennials and the death of the employee engagement survey, *The People Business* is packed full of insight and practical tips – a must-read for any IC professional.' **Helen Deverell, Director, HD Communications**

'I thoroughly recommend reading *The People Business* if you're serious about your communications career. It's packed full of advice and ideas and accurately reflects the vibrancy of working in this field.' **Rachel Miller, Director, All Things IC**

'Every now and then a book appears that has to be read from cover to cover, absorbed and then shared with colleagues and business friends. *The People Business* is one such book.

What hasn't changed in the 55 years I have been involved in the service industry is the huge cost to UK companies and global corporations of losing talented employees and management. My experience has been that 30–40 per cent of all staff turnover could have been prevented had those companies been even vaguely aware of the chasm that existed between the body corporate and its employees.

Not just the Venus and Mars thing. I can remember working with the British subsidiary of an American giant in the cosmetics industry. Staff turnover was abnormally high, with 40 to 50 administrative employees leaving each month out of a department of some 700. It became clear that there was a strong feeling of favouritism and "nationality nepotism". Managers (largely brought over from the US) were seemingly favouring American employees financially, in job allocation and promotions. British staff voted with their feet and senior management had no idea at all that this was happening.

As Personnel and Human Relations became far more professional during the 1980s and 1990s, managing directors and CEOs found a nice "bulwark" against the body of employees and a new source of counsel on employee "demands and needs". But HR has been given few resources to be fully contributory to the health of the business.

Top management were prepared to spend hundreds of thousands on public image and external PR, but virtually ignored their internal reputation.

But here we are in 2017 and there exists too much misunderstanding between top management and its employees.

What this book provides is an opportunity to explore the world of internal communications and discover how reputation management is a brilliant key to ongoing business success.

This is a quite unique book, giving its readers a bird's-eye view of how some famous enterprises, in a splendidly diverse range of sectors, have gained enormously from corporate self-analysis.

Dunstan and Osborne should be commended for a very original and hugely useful publication. I wish I'd had the benefit of their insights 30 years ago.' **Laurence Rosen, Founder and former CEO, Office Angels, and CEO/Chairman of several PR and recruitment companies**

The People Business

The People Business

How ten leaders drive engagement
through internal communications

Annabel Dunstan
Imogen Osborne

KoganPage

First published in Great Britain and the United States in 2017 by Kogan Page Limited

2nd Floor, 45 Gee Street	c/o Martin P Hill Consulting	4737/23 Ansari Road
London EC1V 3RS	122 W 27th St, 10th Floor	Daryaganj
United Kingdom	New York NY 10001	New Delhi 110002
www.koganpage.com	USA	India

© Annabel Dunstan and Imogen Osborne, 2017

The right of Annabel Dunstan and Imogen Osborne to be identified as the authors of this work has been asserted by them in accordance with the Copyright, Designs and Patents Act 1988.

ISBN   978 0 7494 7971 8
E-ISBN   978 0 7494 7972 5

British Library Cataloguing-in-Publication Data

A CIP record for this book is available from the British Library.

Library of Congress Cataloging-in-Publication Data

Names: Dunstan, Annabel, author. | Osborne, Imogen, author.
Title: The people business : how ten leaders drive engagement through internal communications / Annabel Dunstan, Imogen Osborne.
Description: 1st Edition. | New York : Kogan Page Ltd, [2017] | Includes bibliographical references and index.
Identifiers: LCCN 2017024971 (print) | LCCN 2017014147 (ebook) | ISBN 9780749479725 (ebook) | ISBN 9780749479718 (alk. paper)
Subjects: LCSH: Success in business. | Organizational change.
Classification: LCC HF5386 (print) | LCC HF5386 .D846 2017 (ebook) | DDC 658.4/5–dc23

Typeset by Integra Software Services, Pondicherry
Print production managed by Jellyfish
Printed and bound by CPI Group (UK) Ltd, Croydon, CR0 4YY

I would like to dedicate this book to my late father Dr Ivan Dunstan, who led by example and taught me to listen and to seek solutions rather than let things escalate to conflict. He inspired me to overcome obstacles with grace and elegance and above all, to do what I love.

Annabel Dunstan

I'd like to dedicate this book to a special group of people. To my husband, Adrian who called time on me blowing a pea around my desk and encouraged me to do something more productive with my life, to my sons Theo and Riley Peter, good things happen when you hand in your homework on time and to my English teacher, Liz Robinson, who told me to write it all down. I love you all.

Imogen Osborne

CONTENTS

STORIES FROM THE COALFACE

ABOUT THE AUTHORS

Annabel Dunstan

Annabel began her career as a lumberjack's assistant before becoming a ski guide and sailing instructor. She then joined the marketing team at Gulf Air, promoting the Gulf States as a tourism destination at the time of the first Gulf War.

Annabel then joined Le Fevre Communications and cut her teeth on a broad range of clients, handling PR campaigns for Anchor Foods, NatWest Insurance Services, Lloyds TSB, Mortgage Express, Lombard Business Finance and BT.

After the birth of her first child Annabel became a TV presenter fronting 'The Biz' on Six TV, the first regional TV station interviewing CEOs and entrepreneurs on the challenges and opportunities of doing business in Oxfordshire.

With her second born at pre-school, in 2003 Annabel joined 3 Monkeys Communications at launch, on a part-time basis to start, then full time in 2006 as MD overseeing the growth of the award-winning top 50 PR consultancy from £0 to £7.1 million revenues with 65 consultants in central London offices. Clients included Coca-Cola Enterprises, Microsoft, Bic, Calor and Scottish Widows.

Annabel left the jungle in 2011 to found her own consultancy, Gain and Retain, G&R, set up to help businesses that were looking to grow through attracting and growing good people and great clients. This led to a new partnership with Imogen Osborne, former head of global communications, Skype, and founder of QuestionONE. Combining their diagnostic and consultancy skills of G&R a toolkit was co-created to measure and manage client satisfaction and employee engagement: key components of a company's growth. The new company was launched in November 2012: Question and Retain, Q&R.

Imogen Osborne

Imogen has spent over 20 years in the communications industry, working in a range of senior leadership roles at Cisco, Skype, Edelman and WPP.

In 2010, she decided to set up her own company designed to help PR agencies improve the way they manage and measure client satisfaction. A year later, she was re-introduced to Annabel, who had set up her own consultancy business. It quickly became clear that both businesses sat on two sides of the same coin. As the apocryphal story goes, it took 52 minutes to decide a joint future was the brighter future and this culminated in the launch of Q&R (Question and Retain) in 2012. Today, Q&R works with a wide range of clients, from professional services to membership organizations to FMCG companies, helping them listen more effectively to their key stakeholders.

Imogen is a mum, with two gorgeous boys, Theo (aged 17) and Riley Peter (aged 8), and enjoys a lively family life with her husband, Adrian, and his two sons, Louis and Oscar. A passionate follower of film, theatre and live music, she can often be seen dragging any of her nearest and dearest off to see something 'nouveau' in an attempt to propel the senses of perception ever further. In her spare time, she tries to cook and expand her culinary abilities beyond the home baking of muffins.

Bringing *The People Business* to life has been revelatory; it stands out as a genuine achievement and one that will no doubt inspire more books in the future.

CONTRIBUTORS' BIOGRAPHIES

Shiona Adamson, Head of Internal Communication and Communications Services, Natural England

Natural England has 2,000 employees based in locations throughout England. As natural leaders, natural diplomats and natural engineers of landscapes and seas, employees work passionately to create a fair deal for people and nature.

Shiona has over 15 years' UK and international communications experience in the public and private sectors. She's led big and small internal communication teams in-house and as a consultant for Defra, Natural England, Arts Council England, HM Revenue & Customs, Hill & Knowlton, Hewlett-Packard, Novartis, Microsoft, Network Rail, BT and The General Medical Council.

As well as using tried and tested methods to communicate with and engage staff in the workplace, Shiona has increasingly been exploring the use of stories and 'nudges' as ways to inspire behaviour change. By using story-telling techniques – in corporate communication and by coaching leaders in the use of story – Shiona is finding ways to help bring strategy and change to life: making the human connection between people and business. She believes that by experimenting with small acts of kindness by line managers, rather than grand corporate gestures, organizations are much more likely to nudge people in the right direction.

As a mother of two small girls and as a frequent flyer on the trains between Gloucestershire and the rest of the country, Shiona is a huge advocate of agile and virtual working and of Natural England as a pioneer of this approach. She's a great case study/juggler of professional and home life and looks forward to meeting the communication challenges of the future as we welcome more young and 'virtual' people into the workplace.

Jenny Burns, Director of Brand and Customer Experience, Just

Jenny Burns is currently the Brand and Customer Experience Director at Just, a newly merged retirement income specialist, where she is responsible for rebranding the new business. She's passionate about making sure that the business delivers amazing experiences for customers, innovative approaches to problem solving and all things digital.

Jenny started her career at WH Smith, the UK high street retailer, on the management programme. She loved the pace, the direct contact with customers and the thrill of running a business. She was lucky enough to move to the WH Smith head office as a Communications Manager and her addiction to all things communications started there.

Since then, Jenny has had lots of fun in brand, corporate communications and marketing roles at RSA Insurance, Barclays, Centrica British Gas, HBOS and Telefónica O2. For the past 22 years, she has absolutely loved doing what she does across lots of different industries. Over that time Jenny has become what she describes as a positive disrupter; leading the way in making transformational and pioneering changes in well-established businesses.

In 2014, Jenny was named Internal Communications Personality of the Decade by *PR Week*.

Laura Ferguson, People Engagement and Change, BG Group

Laura Ferguson works at senior level as an intercultural change management and communications leader. Her experience has been gained in different industries and geographical regions over the past 20 years. Her passion is helping and supporting the connections between personal goals and aspirations with the how and what of delivery. She is inspired by committed, authentic, interesting people and cultures that adapt, learn and evolve in changing circumstances.

Laura's skills include adaptive thinking and innovation, cross-cultural competency, change management, co-collaboration, communications and engagement. Laura holds a Masters in Intercultural Communications, which she has applied in multiple global change and communications programmes requiring cultural flexibility and understanding.

Laura writes about her experiences of change on www.still-talking.com

Helen den Held, Head of Global Communications, GE Capital

Whilst Helen den Held has earned her stripes on three continents as a global communications leader, her passion lies in coaching and mentoring executives to meet their personal and organizational goals. The only constant in many organizations is change, and ensuring that senior leaders deliver consistent messages that inform, inspire and activate internal and external audiences is crucial. Coaching people through that change is also a prerequisite for success. Facilitating change has become core to the internal communications function and, with her team, Helen implements fully integrated internal and external communications strategies that meet organizational goals and objectives as well as building and improving the company culture.

Helen joined GE Capital, Working Capital Solutions, as Global Head of Communications in January 2015, after returning to the UK from Hong Kong; where she headed up Executive and Internal Communications for the Asia Pacific region for Cisco Systems. Prior to Hong Kong she lived in the Netherlands where she was Head of Brand, Communications and Corporate Social Responsibility for Deloitte.

During her time with Deloitte, she established the Fair Chance Foundation for the firm, a charity that is still focused on coaching and mentoring under-served school-going children. Helen believes in giving back to the community and also serves as a non-executive director on the board of a charity in the housing sector.

Helen was born in Scotland, but she has lived most of her life abroad and completed her Marketing and Communications degrees in South Africa. She is currently following a part-time MSc in Coaching and Behavioural Change at Henley Business School, which will be completed in 2018.

Lindsey Morrell, Head of Global Internal Communications, Telefónica Digital

 Lindsey literally fell into internal communications back in the late 1990s, when a friend approached her about a position going in the IC team in BT and said, 'You'd be good at that,' so she went for an interview, got the job and, as they say, the rest is history.

Her career in IC has spanned nearly 20 years, starting off as an IC adviser in BT, supporting the HR and marketing teams. In 2000, BT announced a restructure across all areas and Lindsey had the opportunity to move across into BT Wireless doing IC. BT Wireless brought together all the company's mobile entities including BT Cellnet (UK), ESAT Digifone (Ireland), Telfort (Netherlands) and Viag Intercom (Germany).

BT Wireless demerged from BT in 2000, and in 2002 it renamed, rebranded and O2 was born. She became IC Manager for O2, then Head of IC for O2 Centre. In 2005 O2 was acquired by the Global Spanish company Telefónica and she became Head of IC for Telefónica Europe until early 2014 when organizational changes in the company meant the dispersal of the European function.

Lindsey now works as part of the wider Global IC team in Telefónica, reporting into the Global IC Director; her role is Head of IC for its digital areas covering consumer, innovation, business solutions, the internet of things, big data and cyber security, amongst others.

Over the years she has had the opportunity to work with many teams across the business, covering a diverse range of IC including change and transformation, Chairman/CEO IC activity programmes, events, intranets, microsites, online publications/newsletters and social media.

Lindsey is married and lives in Surrey with her husband Steve and son Harry.

Suzanne Peck, President, Institute of Internal Communication; Vice President, European Association for Internal Communication (FEIEA); Managing Director, The Sequel Group

Suzanne's internal communication experience spans creating and delivering strategy and communication for leading organizations for more than 25 years.

An award-winning editor, writer and NCTJ-trained journalist, Suzanne began her career working on an evening newspaper as a reporter for four years. She then joined Marks & Spencer working on internal communications projects and as editor of the internal newspaper and magazine, leaving five years later to join Alfred McAlpine as internal communications manager, responsible for a range of communications channels.

Suzanne has worked in internal communications agencies for the past 20 years, creating and delivering communications for a wide range of global clients including Shell, BP, National Grid, Astellas EMEA, and GSK. This work has also involved working at client sites in interim roles to manage communication change projects.

Since 2011 she has been Managing Director of internal communication specialists Sequel Group. As well as managing integrated projects and delivering strategic consultancy and communications training for clients, Suzanne is responsible for day-to-day operations across the business and for strategic planning.

Suzanne is also President of the Institute of Internal Communication (IoIC), a Fellow of the IoIC, and has been a board member of the Institute for more than 15 years. In these voluntary roles, she is an active member in helping the IoIC shape and develop internal communication as well as encouraging new talent into the IC industry. Suzanne is also Vice President of the European Association for Internal Communication (FEIEA) – a pan-European association that aims to raise internal communications standards and communication excellence within Europe.

Norman Pickavance, Leader of the Brand, Innovation & Sustainability Agenda, Grant Thornton

 Norman has spent 30 years helping organizations to transform performance, facilitate change, enable sustainable growth and foster environments of greater trust and integrity.

Over the past 15 years he has been both an executive and non-executive board member of FTSE organizations, central government departments, the NHS and in professional services. Norman has led internal and external communications in complex and demanding environments.

Norman has also developed a parallel career, working with charities in India and co-founding a social enterprise for homeless people in the UK. This experience has led him into policy and advisory work, operating across the political spectrum supporting the former leader of the opposition on zero hour contracts, the former Deputy Prime Minister's policy unit on youth unemployment and working with the Minister of Employment.

In 2014 Norman published a book on the great disconnection that was occurring between business and society and the need to deeply reconnect leaders within organizations to the world around them. The book focused on improving business relevance, reducing risk and delivering on broader corporate responsibilities. Norman was subsequently invited to help implement many of these ideas at Grant Thornton and over the past two years, as a member of the board and partner leading brand innovation and sustainability, has helped to create an exciting new platform for the business through the Vibrant Economy Agenda. This work has seen the formation of a Vibrant Economy Commission, a series of City Live Lab inquiries and the development of a shared enterprise approach in the firm.

Norman is currently acting as a senior adviser to the Blueprint for Better Business on the role of trust and purpose in business.

Fiona Shepherd, CEO of April Six, part of the Mission Group

A seasoned technology marketer with strategic roles on both the client and agency sides, Fiona founded the specialist technology agency April Six 16 years ago. As CEO, Fiona has led the organization through global expansion, extension into PR and, following the acquisition of Proof Communication in 2014, the rebranding of the organization as April Six Proof. She now divides her time across offices in London, San Francisco and Singapore. An experienced creative and commercial innovator, she is embedded in strategic engagement for the agency's global client base and often speaks and publishes on key strategic marketing trends in the global B2B technology sector.

Vickie Sheriff, Director of Communications, Heathrow

Vickie Sheriff is the Director of Campaigns and Communications for Which? the Consumers' Association, a post she took up shortly after the interview for this book was conducted. She was previously Director of Communications at Heathrow, working on the expansion campaign and strategy, and prior to that held a similar role in the global team at drinks giant Diageo plc, which included overseeing employee engagement. Vickie has a long background working in government communications in a variety of departments, from Agriculture to Culture, International Development to Justice, the Treasury to Trade and Industry. Most recently she was Group Director of Communications at the Department for Transport, leading the HS2 campaign and Think! road safety campaigns, and Head of News at No 10 and Deputy Official Spokesman for the Prime Minister.

Besides the day job, Vickie is an Army Reservist and enjoys being in the countryside, horse riding and good company.

Suzie Welch, People Director, PizzaExpress and Jo Harvey, Engagement and Communications Manager, PizzaExpress

  Suzie leads the people function for PizzaExpress, a brand with more than 11,000 employees serving over 31 million customers a year in more than 460 restaurants across the UK. The company's success is based on having the passion and care to consistently deliver delicious, high quality food in sociable, stylish surroundings at value-for-money prices.

People are at the heart of PizzaExpress. High calibre, motivated teams who relish the opportunities and challenges that the company presents work hard to develop the PizzaExpress experience, both in the UK and overseas. Suzie works globally to ensure that the right people are in the right roles as the company grows and that they continue to harness the culture and values that have been in the business since it started 51 years ago.

Suzie joined the PizzaExpress team after 17 years at Whitbread in a number of operational and HR roles, working across a number of brands including Costa Coffee and TGI Fridays.

She believes that for any business with people-centric core values, engagement and communications are key. Suzie is passionate about using communication to enable team members to build emotional connections and work collaboratively to deliver high performance and engaged teams.

Suzie lives in Cambridgeshire with her husband and two children, and has a passion for cooking for friends and family.

Jo Harvey has been passionate about the hospitality industry from a young age and is on a mission to prove what a rewarding and satisfying career choice it can be for school leavers and graduates alike. Great internal communications play a huge role in this – not only sharing the values and beliefs of the organization but also providing inspiring and motivating communications that help build a great team and a productive culture.

Jo has worked in all areas of the hospitality industry: a commis waiter, operational management, external communication and, most recently, internal communications for organizations such as Conran Restaurants Ltd, Villandry, Ping Pong, Bumpkin and PizzaExpress Ltd.

She can mostly be found eating her way around the world, particularly in her corner of West London.

FOREWORD

In June 2016, the PRCA (Public Relations & Communications Association) published the PR Census, revealing that the UK PR industry is worth £12.9 billion – over £3 billion more than in 2013. Part of this growth has been driven by a balance between the new and traditional ways of communicating. In other words, clients want to stay ahead and to stay in touch with all of their audiences, regardless of what communications medium they prefer.

In this new world of communicating, which one might validly call 'The digital age', there is a blurring of the lines between what is shared internally and externally. Today, everything a company says is public information, and everything a company does is up for critical review. The world of PR is colliding with the world of internal communications (IC). As curators of content, senior communications professionals are keen to create a sustainable and authentic conversation across a diverse group of stakeholders. With this comes, of course, a wide range of challenges and opportunities to be creative. There is a real hunger to innovate, not least because of the variety of new technologies available. Some of the stories you will read here will give you excellent inspiration for introducing new tricks and tools into your communications approach.

What drew me to this book, *The People Business,* is its goal of sharing best practice on how to manage your communications under the spotlight. I use the term 'communications' in its broadest sense, because the discipline of IC is changing irrevocably – an opinion endorsed by every interviewee. Whether you're leading IC, or preparing for the launch of the century, the pathway to engaging successfully with your audiences lies within these pages. Our experienced communications leaders will tell you candidly what good looks like, and what they've learnt at the coalface. They have shared generously and deeply, so you will feel enriched and better prepared for the communications challenges you face.

I've spent nearly 20 years in the communications industry, and if I have one observation to make it is that an honest and open conversation with any type of stakeholder will always yield insight. As the Director General of a professional body I have to embrace all types of feedback – good and bad. What makes my job easier is when I can find quick ways to improve a member's experience. My counsel to you therefore is to use this book to draw up your smart list of what to do quickly and professionally when things go awry, as they so often do. Equally, when the day is done and the sun is setting, take some time to invest in your intellectual capital, and to absorb the strategic value and 'know how' that the interviewees have shared as part of their journeys.

I have thoroughly enjoyed reading *The People Business*. It's a must-have for any senior communications professional, and will be an excellent resource to draw on when one of any of the stories included suddenly becomes resonant to you.

Francis Ingham
Director General of the Public Relations & Communications
  Association
Chief Executive of the International Communications Consultancy
  Organisation (ICCO)
Master of the City of London Company of Public Relations
  Practitioners

ACKNOWLEDGEMENTS

We would like to thank all our interviewees who gave their valuable time to talk through their thoughts and experiences with us and without whom we simply would not have a book at all.

We would also like to mention all of our clients engaged in measuring and managing internal communications and employee sentiment because without them, we would not have a business.

An essential part of the editing process has been led by Piers Ford, freelance journalist, writer and training consultant who is both our colleague and friend of many years. Piers has helped us curate the reams of interview transcripts into a coherent form and brought to life the broad spectrum of experience and insights shared by all of our interviewees.

Our thanks also go to Ellwood Atfield, the IC recruitment specialists and Liam FitzPatrick, founder of Working Communications, for co-hosting our now legendary Internal Communications Fight Club events where the great and the good get feisty over topical IC issues of the day. These debates have not only shaped the rationale for *The People Business* but encouraged us to explore the wealth of IC approaches alive today.

We are particularly grateful to Francis Ingham, Director General, Public Relations & Communications Association (PRCA) and Chief Executive of the International Communications Consultancy Organisation (ICCO) for his constant support for Question & Retain. Francis has been a continual source of inspiration for us both in terms of growing our business and opening doors that would otherwise have been closed.

We would also like to thank our two business advisers, mentors and friends Ian Henderson, Executive Creative Director and Chairman, AML Group, and BJ Cunningham, owner of BJ Cunningham Ltd, who provide sage counsel and keep us sane. They too continue to be extremely generous in giving their time, despite being very busy people themselves.

We must also acknowledge Charlotte Owen, Development Editor, and Jenny Volich, Commissioning Editor, at our publishers Kogan Page, who have helped us steer a steady course throughout this whole book process. They have cheered and chivvied us along the way and kept a steady hand on meeting editorial deadlines, which has been incredibly useful.

And finally to my co-founder and friend, Imogen Osborne, who elegantly brought the themes of our book together in the Introduction and Summary chapters. It's been a journey! And likewise to my co-founder and friend, Annabel Dunstan whose inclusive personality and unbridled energy inspired this book and ensured the printer met the page.

Introduction

Why should you read this book?

In the next 173 pages, we will be looking at the evolution of internal communications (IC) from a once poor relation of the communications mix to becoming a respected discipline in its own right. To illustrate this transformation, we have devoted 10 chapters of this book to understanding what good looks like when it comes to the practice of IC. Our interviews span a range of blue-chip companies and the Institute of Internal Communication (IOIC). Each chapter tells the individual story of how IC is making a difference in industries such as the food and leisure sector, creative communications, oil and gas industry, travel and professional services by drawing on the experiences of senior IC practitioners who have 'seen it all'.

We hope, as you turn the pages, you will discover new ideas and inspiration from some of the UK's senior communications leaders, all of whom are working at the coalface of IC. Their roles are finely balanced between helping the organizations they work for find a 'voice' and ensuring that when the organization speaks, it does so credibly and with emotional authenticity.

What is the state of IC today?

Before we begin our journey of discovery, we should acknowledge that some companies are proving to be particularly good at IC. They seem able to grasp the nettle of how to communicate and converse with their workforce with the right level of passion. So what is driving this and how are they doing it?

Looking at the companies profiled in this book, we find some of the routes to success are achieved through breaking with tradition and insisting that the organization throw out old habits and embrace the new. For example, a prevailing theme is the death of the annual engagement survey, which we will explore in more detail later on in this chapter. Another predominant theme is the rise of the employer brand because it is the glue that holds everything and everyone together during periods of organizational change.

That said, while the companies we have chosen to profile have a particular success story to share, not all companies are ready to break through to this new ground. Many still struggle with the need to 'open the corporate kimono' and bare all, believing this level of transparency will disengage its workforce rather than unite them. Each company we have profiled can attest that success takes time and is not without plenty of challenges along the way. We will look at these challenges in the chapters ahead and explore how they are being overcome.

Whatever your business, we believe it is a universal truth that companies need to wear a new hat of responsibility and honesty when it comes to communicating with staff. For some this comes naturally because it is seen as a necessity if the desired business goals are to be achieved. The more you know, the more you can grow as the adage goes, and while that may seem simplistic, it is fundamentally true.

So for the businesses that are comfortable with increased transparency and candour, the role of IC is pivotal. This is where IC as an emergent and powerful communications discipline can really prove its value. In other words, if there is a discipline in communications that is 'on the up', it is internal communications. What is interesting is the 'how' and the 'what' that is precipitating this change.

The evolving role of IC

The IoIC (Institute of Internal Communication) states the following:

> The Internal Communications profession – whether in a small not for profit, a giant global enterprise or a sprawling local community – should manage the understanding and knowledge that binds the individuals in the organization together. Just as marketing sprang from sales and

advertising in the 1940s and 1950s to become a board role, so internal communication is finding its professional feet. It's no longer the poor cousin of public relations, the off-shoot of human resources or corporate communication. It now has a place at the top table.

That's fighting talk. When we correlate this with the way business operates today, it is clear that successful IC is no longer measured by sending out an internal newsletter or an e-mail from the CEO. It is far more sophisticated and spoiled by the increase in new tools to help IC tell its story. Some of these tools take the form of innovative technologies and others come down to how you exploit face-to-face interaction, which is by far the most preferred IC vehicle. Talking with staff, having an open conversation works. Yet there are techniques to 'getting this right' when it comes to the tone of the discussion and it takes time to find your voice.

Today, businesses of varying shapes and sizes know that it is no longer simply enough to give someone a role in their organization and expect them to get on with their job safe in the knowledge that they understand the overall direction of the company. No matter how large or small your company is, people like to know what's going on. And they expect information or news to be shared regularly and in a digestible format that is not locked in corporate-speak but cuts through the verbiage.

However, the complexities of doing business in a global or domestic market require definition internally and nuancing with those who might not be customer-facing but form part of the all-important 'back office' support. This is easier said than done. Couple this with the predominance of the internet: we know that people can often find out what's happening just by simply going online. Then there is the expectation that information from the company you work for should come quickly and not be held back. A failure to do so results in outcry. This needs no better stage than an instant messaging platform that all too readily captures the emotion and real-time sentiment of those impacted.

Bottom line? The days of the memo are over and, on many occasions, people already know what's going on before you actually tell them.

So how does all of this impact internal communications?

The answer is: a lot. This book will grapple with some of the very real issues of communicating, especially when the company is in a constant state of flux. In fact, every individual we spoke to claimed their organization was in a perpetual state of change. Some of this is driven by market factors, some of it by organizational structure and some of it just by the very raison d'être of the company's mission to become famous.

The IoIC offers a clear definition of what IC is today; it is as an 'enabling function – it makes your organization work… the oil that helps smooth the running of your organization or a bridge that creates links between people and functions'. The IoIC goes on further to state that 'there is an increasingly well-understood link between communication, engagement and organizational success'.

As part of the research process in preparing for this book, Question & Retain (Q&R) ran a Pulse Check™ (an intuitive, online software tool that take the 'pulse' of how people are feeling about any topic), asking for senior IC practitioners' views on how IC is perceived today. The feedback was compelling, delivering the insights shown in Figure 0.1.

IC gaining credibility

Starting with the top statistic in terms of IC gaining credibility, Vickie Sheriff, in the chapter on Heathrow, observes that IC was traditionally the Cinderella of the communications disciplines. In her view, it has simply been used as a mechanism to 'get the message out' but now, thanks to the arrival of more, high calibre individuals in influential communications roles (that have both budget and remit to effect change), the role of IC is changing for the better. Sheriff's observation underlines the goal of this book and in particular how seasoned communicators are leveraging their skills sets to 're-invent' IC as a credible and powerful communications discipline.

It doesn't just come down to how the messages or the content are delivered. Time and emphasis need to be spent on perfecting the

Figure 0.1   How IC is perceived today

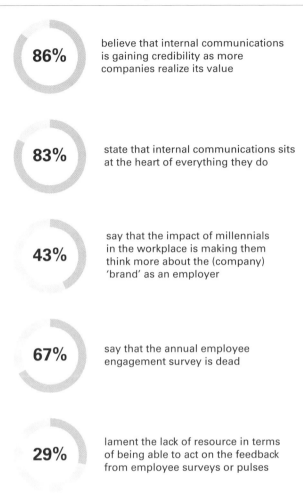

86% believe that internal communications is gaining credibility as more companies realize its value

83% state that internal communications sits at the heart of everything they do

43% say that the impact of millennials in the workplace is making them think more about the (company) 'brand' as an employer

67% say that the annual employee engagement survey is dead

29% lament the lack of resource in terms of being able to act on the feedback from employee surveys or pulses

right 'tone' and making sure that while you are sharing information, employees remain part of the conversation. In fact at the point at which the information is shared, there is a switch from broadcast to engagement and people start talking to each other, regardless of job title or seniority.

It makes for a refreshing change from the old days of simply sending the news out and expecting people to read and digest it without requiring any further context or humanization. Sheriff goes on to assert that the bigger role for IC is to be the mouthpiece for the company's vision and bring it alive, using the right tools that guarantee the truth will not be diluted. Equally these tools are charged with encouraging the right kind of interactions from those who are on the listening end of the communications pipe.

IC sits at the heart of everything we do

If further proof were needed that IC is an emergent tour de force in today's working environment, you only have to look at the prevailing view from our Pulse that shows 83 per cent state that IC sits at the heart of everything they do. IC is no longer seen as an 'add-on' function nor does it sit with HR. IC is right in the middle of everything, or at least that is where it should live.

In the chapter on Heathrow, Sheriff talks about a 'visual culture' where IC can build or paint a picture of what is now and what will happen next so that employees can see as well as hear what their future will be. This evolution of IC is reaffirmed by Laura Ferguson, Head of People Engagement and Change at BG Group/Shell, who describes in detail the emergence of the 'employer brand' and heralds a new era in how companies must work to ensure their internal perception is as strong as their external perception as the two are inextricably linked.

As part of our research for this book, we looked at the five IC trends to watch according to Newsweaver (https://www.newsweaver. com/five-internal-communication-trends-to-watch-in-2016/#. WD1kOTvPxhs). These are discussed below.

1. 360° measurement

The methodology used must be 360 and square off all bases. It is vital to present the 'whole' picture ie by location, channel, department, audience, age, role, etc so that the business can understand where its strengths and weaknesses lie.

2. Engaging all generations

It is a brave new world of communications. Companies today have a wide range of age groups and they all have preferred methods for interaction. Striking a balance here is key to ensuring people's preferences are respected.

3. Working remotely

In the United States alone, remote working has grown by 103 per cent since 2005 and 6.5 per cent in 2014. Studies repeatedly show employees are now not at their desk 50–60 per cent of the time. The number of people working from home is on the increase in the United Kingdom, according to the CBI. A total of 59 per cent of employers who responded to a survey in 2011 were offering teleworking, up from 13 per cent in 2006.

Worldwide, more than 50 per cent of people who telecommute part-time said they wanted to increase their remote hours. Additionally, 79 per cent of knowledge workers in a global survey by PGI said they work from home, and 60 per cent of remote workers in the survey said that, if they could, they would leave their current job for a full-time remote position at the same pay rate (Source: remote.co).

Many Fortune 1000 companies are in the midst of completely overhauling their work spaces around the fact that employees are already mobile. Internal communicators must now tackle the challenge of removing barriers for their mobile workers. Whether 'remote' is offsite, the factory floor, in the car or the home office – they all need to feel connected and engaged with internal communications.

4. Multichannel is the new black

According to Newsweaver, 'One method of communication in an organization is never enough. Employees have channel preferences plus there are routes more suited for certain types of messaging than others.' Set this against the generational diversity in the workplace and it's clear that internal communications channels need to play to their strengths and be an integral part of the whole. They cannot run in isolation and need to have a specific role to be successful. They also need a senior IC practitioner to guide when and where they are deployed.

5. The perfect package

Successful IC is no longer about making isolated announcements on e-mail or simply pushing out company updates at the behest of the senior management team. People want to know the WIIFM (What's In It For Me?) factor and to feel involved. And that's where story-telling comes to life.

These trends show how much IC is expanding as a communications discipline and has many tricks up its sleeve. They suggest IC must diversify in lock step with its audiences as they vary by geography and culture. The critical success factor lies with innovation – examples of which we will focus on in the coming chapters – because it is this kind of thinking that has transformed companies and enabled them to achieve tangible commercial success.

Impact of millennials

Possibly one of the more emotive areas for discussion is the impact millennials are having in the workplace: 43 per cent of those people we pulsed said that the impact of millennials in the workplace was making them think more about the (company) 'brand' as an employer. It is generally agreed that millennials are more motivated by values and want to be part of delivering the message rather than to sit on the side-lines and be 'talked at'. Equally important for them is being part of the conversation and able to speak freely and with candour. A respondent to our Pulse Check™ (Figure 0.1) remarks that the arrival of millennials in the workplace is:

> Making us think more about our 'brand' as an employer. Millennials are increasingly informed and opinionated about brands generally and their expectation of their employer and what they stand for even higher. We have to address that to be able to recruit and retain millennials who are very important for a creative industry.

For some, this can feel like revolt inside a company that has conservative roots. For others, it is a breath of fresh air and is encouraging everyone to 're-think' the way they judge scenarios or make decisions.

In his TED Talk on 'What makes companies fail', Knut Haanaes, Senior Partner at the Boston Consulting Group, hones it down to one factor. 'The mark of a great company,' he says, 'is to constructively challenge what it is doing.' So perhaps this is the role of millennials – to ensure that the company of today invites feedback from its people in its purest form, unfiltered and constructive. It is down to Generation Y to make this a common behaviour.

It is accepted now that individuals, of all backgrounds and disciplines, look to the companies they work for to be 'different' today in the way they interact with their staff, customers and suppliers. However, many companies are still restrained by politics and incumbent processes that slow their businesses down. In this scenario, IC has a pivotal role to play. It is the job of IC to build a powerful narrative around what makes the company so special. This narrative binds people together, gives them a sense of direction and purpose and a role to play in the making of something great and good for all.

Some companies are fortunate in that they can offer other incentives. Whether it's the draw of a great working environment, opportunities to work abroad or from home, the ability to take a step back from the 'day job' and enjoy some creative thinking space – there are plenty of benefits to take advantage of. There is also the freedom to speak one's mind in public forums as people are more empowered now and have an expectation of what their employee experience should be. With millennials this is especially true, and companies both today and in the future will have to factor in their impact on how they behave both externally and internally.

We also know that the rise of millennials in the workplace, who are seemingly genetically programmed to challenge the status quo, are having a significant impact on how IC develops as a discipline. Whether that comes down to how senior leaders are coached to ensure they speak with authenticity or how news is shared internally, the fact is that with millennials in the workplace, the communications environment changes dynamically. Corporate-speak becomes a poor cousin to honesty and clarity. While some argue that people don't need to know everything, whatever is shared internally needs to be credible and hold weight.

The annual engagement survey is dead

It will come as no surprise as we live in a 24 x 7 world in terms of news that 67 per cent of those we pulsed said that the annual employee engagement survey is dead. We can see how old habits of the past are being thrown to one side in favour of faster, more intuitive ways to engage. The perennial (and often tedious) annual engagement survey has run its course. No one will miss the 72+ question surveys that ploughed through every inch of the organization's fabric asking for feedback on the appraisal process, facilities, working relationships, etc. These surveys (which took nearly an hour to complete) and then the results (if they were shared) would come back often three months later, once they had been synthesized to highlight the positives and make brief mention of where things needed to be fixed. As one of our respondents observed:

> (Annual) employee surveys are a thing of the past and don't respond to the needs of employees or businesses quick enough anymore. By the time you've done the survey, analysed the results and presented all that to leaders, the world has moved on. We need something faster and employees and leaders need to take more accountability for their own engagement and that of their teams. Internal social sentiment might be the way forward.

What is intriguing is that our stories from the coalface will confirm that this isn't just one industry sector that's saying that annual employee engagement surveys hold no currency within their organizations now. This is cross-sector and it is marking a new era in internal communications and a great opportunity for innovation.

Acting on the feedback

Every organization we have spoken to as a result of writing this book has been very clear on how well it acts on the feedback from all or any type of employee engagement. Almost a third (29 per cent) say they do act on the feedback but not everything gets done straight away. Equally 29 per cent say they need more time and resource to do this properly and if IC has a challenge ahead, it is how it can streamline how and when the results are shared.

For some companies, especially those operating globally, reaching everyone within a realistic timeframe is the first hurdle to jump over. Then it comes down to what you are sharing and how this can be 'personalized'. Everyone agrees that face-to-face interaction is by far the best way to communicate with staff. In tandem with this is providing a 'platform' whereby people can access information and contribute if they wish. It is a fine balance and one we will explore further in the chapters ahead.

Tips for success

During these interviews, we asked each of our interviewees to share their top tips for success in IC. Over and over again the need to really understand the strategic direction of the business was seen as essential. The more you are able to get under the skin of an organization and really feel its heart beat, the more in tune you will be with the overall strategy and trajectory. After all, it is the business strategy that defines the tone of voice and the language you can adopt when explaining what's going on. Grandiose words such as 'company narrative' are familiar friends with commercial strategy, but strip away the corporate-speak and you will find it makes sense in telling the company story and evolving it. Everyone wants to know where they are going – not least so they can decide if they want to go there.

Measurement – everyone's favourite topic

One of the ongoing challenges for IC is how it proves its worth beyond, in its simplest terms, the 'wordship' of speech writing or the realm of internal newsletters. Of the companies we talked to, many deploy a variety of measurement tools and methodologies that include online polling, calls with site and engagement leaders, face-to-face meetings and regular 'temperature' checks.

The goal is to track sentiment on an ongoing basis and benchmark the results. It is also important that the data that comes back is not just reported as numbers on a pie chart: it needs to explain what's going on in the business and highlight issues/concerns as well as opportunities to grow. The skill therefore is in how the data is interpreted in terms of understanding overall sentiment and what implications this has for the business. Benchmarking over time also provides a solid framework to understand the data and see where the opportunities are within the business to either spend more time explaining and discussing what the organization is aspiring to achieve or identifying new ways to inspire employees.

That said, gathering rafts of feedback is the easy part of the exercise. Most employees are keen to share their views and give their feedback – constructive or otherwise. The key is how you act on the data quickly and take positive action. Companies can become obsessive about information and find themselves under-resourced when it comes to dealing with the glut of data. This sets businesses up for failure because they become locked in analysis and miss the opportunity to demonstrate to employees that they are listening and acting on the feedback.

As our Pulse Check™ confirms, 29 per cent say their organizations lack the necessary resource to act on their data. This is the perennial challenge of the annual engagement survey – there is just too much information that comes back and too little time to do anything really productive with it. More often than not, because there is so much to digest, it takes a long time to process. Once you arrive at the point of reviewing the results, the feedback is usually weeks if not months out of date.

The lesson that many companies are learning is that a 'less is more' approach is the answer. Ask less and have more time to act on what you hear back is the mantra. The more you are seen to be acting on what your employees are telling you, the more people believe they are being listened to. This sits at the heart of a successful engagement path and gives IC the power to 'report back' on what the company has done. In other words, tell us what's on your mind and we will do something about it.

When IC is diluted

While we will be focusing on best practice in this book when it comes to successful internal communications, it is worth casting an eye over what doesn't work well when communicating with employees.

Some of our interviews have alluded to the need to educate senior management on how to communicate. There is a clear need to guard against CEOs promoting their self-interest and their own agenda because people will see through this. Nothing disengages an employee more quickly than when the real issues of the day are passed over for a pitch on the vision, mission and values. There is a line between leadership using IC as a mouthpiece for the organization and an opportunity to have a conversation.

Simply put, there is no point paying lip service to the discipline of internal communications. People want to hear an authentic voice and one that doesn't rely on prescribed messages or a scripted agenda. They want the truth and they want access to those who make the bigger decisions for the company. They want to tell them what's working and what's not and to be able to do this without recrimination or marking their card as a 'disruptive' employee. This can make for a lively internal environment, but if employees are able to embrace all feedback and conversations in the understanding that this will help build the bigger company they are striving for, then let this be a constant flow throughout the organization.

The rise of the employer brand

Businesses in turn are recognizing that their 'brand' as an employer, while alluring from an external perspective, has to permeate through every touch-point with the employee. The employee experience begins at the point of recruitment and passes through interacting with the sales team, understanding product development, negotiating remuneration and going through the appraisal process.

As a result, companies are beginning to place a lot more emphasis on and investment in the recruitment process so they can build a positive profile and one that resonates with today's hires as well as tomorrow's. Active engagement starts at the moment at which the employee walks through the door and on to when they leave the building and head home to their families and friends. It is as if the employee has become the 'internal' customer and his or her overall engagement and happiness has a profound and ongoing impact on how an organization is perceived and its ability to thrive.

Moreover, loyalty has a new currency in terms of staff retention: it's no longer enough to pay the most, you have to be prepared to do the right thing to keep people engaged. In other words, people are now motivated by different things. Some companies are exploiting this by creating positive differences to the employee journey. Sometimes that represents itself in the way a company chooses to listen to its staff. Working Capital Solutions, part of GE Capital, has a system called 'Seat Rides', which allows its employees to sit next to the senior leadership team and see what their day is like. Perceptions of senior management as being aloof are eschewed for a more realistic view of what really happens and the amount of responsibility that comes with the job.

In March 2016, Q&R ran an industry-wide Pulse Check™ across the HR and recruitment communities. It asked how much influence the external profile of their senior management team had on their recruitment process: 67 per cent claimed it has a lot of influence with a further 29 per cent saying it has some influence on the recruitment process but will have more in the future. As one respondent commented, 'As more organizations use social media to raise the external profile of their businesses, and more candidates engage with online search facilities to do research prior to interviewing/joining an organization, this area will become more prominent.'

A creative culture – what good looks like

In his book, *Creativity, Inc*, Ed Catmull charts the success of Pixar as a result of engaging effectively with its employees. In actual fact, what Pixar did in terms of communicating inside its walls broke many traditions of hierarchy. It began with uniting people with a common goal – the joyousness of the story-telling – and this was done unilaterally across the company, regardless of role or title.

As Catmull attests, 'Engaging the collective brain power of the people you work with is an active, ongoing process.' This approach transcends every process within a company – from hiring to retaining staff and keeping them inspired and engaged along the way. When hiring, Catmull observed the following was essential: 'give them potential to grow more weight to their current skills level. What they will be capable of tomorrow is more important than what they can do today'.

There is no doubt that Pixar has risen to become a widely admired and respected company and also very profitable. For IC to be successful, senior leaders need to see the impact on the bottom line. Perhaps the learning here is that to achieve this, you need a sum of many processes coming together. For example, working in a 'no blame' culture is essential to build trust and cooperation between all. Catmull supports this in his book: 'The desire for everything to run smoothly is a false goal. It leads to measuring people by the mistakes they make rather than their ability to solve problems.' In the same way, how new ideas are handled is critical to the engagement process. The concept of empowering teams to challenge the status quo and overrule it with new thinking is powerful. It comes with risks, but if nurtured in the right way the numbers will tell the rest of the story.

Conclusion

Ahead of you lie stories from the coalface, told by senior IC practitioners whose job it is to wrestle with a multiplicity of challenges every day. They have been candid and happy to share their insights on what good looks like in terms of managing millennials, building an employer brand, avoiding message dilution, being ruthless when acting on the feedback and kicking out old traditions in favour of the new.

They are practised and professional and smart enough to know every organization has its limits. Sometimes the job is about realizing your potential and working out the smartest way to get there, even if your culture will never come close to that of seismic brands such as Nike, Lego or Apple. As we know, every individual has a view or opinion and what works for one may not work for many and vice versa. The art is in how you tell your company story and keep people interested along the way, prompting the question: what does successful IC look like today and how do leaders drive engagement? We hope you will find the answers to this in our book.

Thank you.

Reference

Catmull, E with Wallace, A (2014) *Creativity, Inc: Overcoming the unseen forces that stand in the way of true inspiration,* Random House, London

Telefónica Digital

01

How a culture of openness and transparency ensures that employees feel constantly up-to-date with internal change and the impact of external influences in a highly regulated business

LINDSEY MORRELL

Head of Global Internal Communications, Telefónica Digital

Lindsey Morrell came to the discussion steeped in experience both as a leader and in the rich, granular skill set of the professional IC practitioner. What sets her apart is that most of that experience has been gleaned within a single industry: telecommunications, starting out in BT, then O2 and now Telefónica, the telecoms giant. Today, she is head of internal communications for Telefónica Digital.

In her 18 years within IC she has also fulfilled a number of key roles at a regional and local level. During that time, the business itself has gone through many shifts and changes, shaped and occasionally buffeted by the boisterous climate of the international telecoms industry. It's impossible to conceive that there is any aspect of the operation that has not been influenced by the many internal campaigns she has led, which – as she told us ahead of our conversation – have embraced every kind of bespoke initiative and event, been based on clear messaging above all else, and have focused on engaging Telefónica people in the company story, strategy, objectives and vision.

Changing attitudes

Lindsey started by explaining how she has noticed a sea change in the attitude towards IC from leadership teams and directors. When she was setting out on her career, many companies simply didn't have an IC function. It fell within the remit of the PR or HR teams, and just kind of blended into an amorphous cloud of internal and employee comms – a perception that probably still lingers in some organizations. Lindsey is adamant that they are in fact two separate functions: employee comms are indeed driven by HR, as well as the individual employee, and focus primarily on operational matters such as holidays, salaries, payroll, sick-pay and bonuses. IC, on the other hand, focuses on company strategy, purpose, goals and direction – the things your people need to know. It's the latter which, increasingly, is better understood as a function in its own right – not something that is vaguely attributed to HR. It has a direct impact on the bottom line, and it acknowledges employees' roles as ambassadors. The more they know, Lindsey told us, the more they understand about the direction the company is taking, the more they can be true and valuable advocates for the business.

The idea that IC can really add value to the business is relatively new, but it has gained genuine currency at the top table. This is filtering down through the organization to the extent that people will call upon IC services for support in delivering a plethora of campaigns and messages, via a full range of traditional and digital channels: branding, events, forums, town halls, Yammer, social media, the intranet, newsletters, bulletins, videos and animations. In short, said Lindsey, it's no longer just about copywriting. IC can work with many different teams, departments and business roles across the company – and this acceptance is the biggest change she has sensed in her career so far.

Annabel: Can you describe how internal comms sits within Telefónica?

Lindsey: Within Telefónica there is a global internal communications function that sits in head office in Madrid. We also work closely with our operating businesses across the globe. Within those, we also have internal communications teams. So, it's very much a virtual matrix working set-up. For example, we have an IC team in Germany, which would look after all the local assets for internal communication, and what's happening there, the CEO in Germany, his actual internal activity plan – all the things that are happening on the ground that affect people in their business.

We link in with local teams when anything comes from a global perspective that we want all of our employees to know about or participate in, whether it's a big campaign or initiative. I would help them to understand the overall context, provide them with the key messages, branding, banners and headers. Then they would launch it at a local level.

That happens with all of our businesses across Latin America, where we have a huge presence. We are present in 21 countries worldwide, most of them in Latin America, including Brazil, Argentina and Mexico. Many of them have their own internal communications teams working to get all of our global campaigns out across the business.

Annabel: How many people and resources are given to IC?

Lindsey: There are currently around 20 of us in the global team, which sits in our main hub in Madrid. Some of the team are dedicated to IT-based comms, looking after the global intranet and the web, and focusing on day-to-day visual campaigns and things like that. The rest of the team are either IC business partners who look after key areas across the organization and work across different channels, or those working on key projects as required, eg the launch of a new global recognition programme, or the launch of a quarterly pulse survey. They are responsible for building and delivering the overall communications plan, and across the business people use our services to support and deliver their specific campaigns and events.

Across the local teams, it depends on how big that business is. In the UK we've got 6,700 employees and a relatively small team of around eight internal communicators. But somewhere like Paraguay or Uruguay, which is a comparatively small business, there might just be one person who deals with the internal communications, because the actual employee base is that much smaller and there's not a requirement for such a big IC team.

Annabel: What are the challenges of millennials and Gen Z in the workplace for you?

Lindsey: We've been talking about millennials for a long while. Over the years, Telefónica has very much shown itself to be a cool company to work for – and a lot of people have worked there for a long time. Four or five years ago, there was a real push to get some younger people into the business, bringing both fresh blood and fresh thinking. We set up various initiatives and programmes, including one which is all about young start-ups coming into the business and helping them to find sponsors who will give them a certain level of financial support. They don't necessarily work for Telefónica.

In fact, there is now a pile of activity that we do around young people. We invest a lot in millennials. IC is heavily involved in 'One Young World', an initiative where we take about 30 young graduates from the business and get them to participate in a forum. It's akin to a United Nations – bringing loads of our young people together to talk about various initiatives and campaigns, and about bigger world issues. In our UK business, we started a programme called 'Think Big', which is very much directed at young people and helping them to realize their full potential. We help them launch ideas and programmes that use technology to benefit the places. However, I do think that maybe we're using the word 'millennial' to death, and sometimes we might be too specific about the initiatives that have been targeted at that audience. We've had some feedback from our other employees, asking why we do campaigns or activities directed solely at this group of people. After all, it's not just that particular generation that can be entrepreneurial, have a different outlook about the way things should be run, or bring different insights to the table. You can be 45 or 50 years old, and still be very tech-savvy and know what's going on. So perhaps our focus shouldn't just be targeted specifically at the 'millennial' audience.

On the other hand, we do have quite a lot of fresh, young people in the business. And that's why we have our own millennial network, driven by the growing number of young people, which is about encouraging everyone to share their experiences. But I think we now need to look at what we mean by 'millennial'. Is it less about age and more about a particular mindset or attitude? We're working on a campaign at the moment focused on this actual topic, and we're doing plenty of things around it to collect and gauge people's responses.

Rebooting perceptions

So according to Lindsey, 'millennial' is a phrase that is overdue for a reboot – and we thought this highly significant coming from a telecoms industry insider. The sector is among the most regulated in the world; perhaps one of the main reasons why, despite the rapid advances of underlying technologies, it is also often perceived as a very traditional business to work in, where checks and balances are always intervening to hamper creativity. Lindsey's observation refutes that clichéd view. More importantly, it also throws down the challenge for an IC practitioner in any sector to take a long hard look at the accumulated received wisdom on best practice, and challenge the very language that we use to label our most common tropes.

Visions of trust

This plays out in some interesting ways when it comes to looking at the requirement for transparency. Regulation, she pointed out to us, has constantly been part and parcel of the telecom company's existence. As each new phase of technology comes forward, things like spectrum, consolidation, 4G and 5G all bring new possibilities for the mining and exploitation of Big Data. With that wealth of customer data, the big question that telecoms companies like Telefónica must address is how to monetize it while retaining the all-important trust of the customers who have provided it. The need to establish trust boundaries within its networks while being innovative in how it charges for its services and bills people, means that there will be some interesting challenges around branding and engagement messaging for the IC in the not-so-distant future. With that in mind, we wanted to know Lindsey's thoughts on the annual employee engagement survey – and were left in no doubt about her vision: that pulse surveys, with their flexibility, versatility and capacity for timeliness, are the future.

Annabel: Do you believe the annual employee engagement survey is dead?

Lindsey: One hundred per cent yes. We've always done an annual engagement survey, for many, many years. I think for a lot of big companies there is a legacy issue that means an annual employment survey is still the way things are done. But with a single survey I just don't feel you can gauge what people are thinking, and how they're feeling, because when they're doing the survey, they will answer those questions according to how they're feeling on that particular day.

So, if the survey is carried out in the first four or five months of the year when everything's been great and they've seen some brilliant campaigns, they've had training and development, that's one thing. But what if it's later, when they're not having such a good time and things aren't working out. Everything affects how they will respond to those questions. That's why I think it's difficult to really gauge how your workforce is feeling if you're just doing one survey a year. Having said that, we have reduced our survey dramatically over time, from around 100 questions to 70, then 50. At the moment it's down to just over 30 questions.

We are also now doing quarterly polls and I think that is definitely the way to go: smaller, more regular surveys with different demographics, and not using the same audience each time. With pulse surveys you don't need to target the whole of your employee base. You can just choose your demographics and then run it with smaller groups. This means that, suddenly, you're getting a steady representative drip-feed of views from a wide sample of people, four to six times a year. I believe you're going to get a much truer picture of how your employees really feel about the company, its strategy, and whether or not they feel they're moving in the right direction. The annual survey just doesn't give you the real qualitative data you need to be able to test how your workforce is feeling.

Annabel: You mentioned earlier that IC now has a place at the top table. How do you prove whether it's working? And how do you measure the impact of internal comms?

Lindsey: We have various mechanisms in place. We have a survey that we send out to some of our key stakeholders to find out how they feel about our internal communications. But I think one of the key things that demonstrates IC having that leverage of being at the top table and being listened to, is how effective your directors and your CEO end up being.

For example, you might have a CEO who just does a few announcements a year, in the traditional way. But if the IC function has the ear of the board, you can end up with your chairperson, CEO and directors all doing Yammer debates, coffee mornings, open forums, town halls, and being involved in all of those more face-to-face activities. And I think that would be the clearest demonstration of the impact that internal communications is now having – if you can get those people away from their desks, walking the talk and listening to people. The key is to inspire them to want to listen to people and know what employees are thinking or feeling. They might feel that they're doing something completely strange or wrong to begin with, but once they get used to listening, they can change their attitude.

It's all about getting your directors to actually do a lot more communication across different channels – they don't necessarily have to be face-to-face. We have Yammer groups and encourage our directors to get involved. Sometimes the initial feedback is along the lines of, 'Oh, well, there doesn't seem to be a lot of activity. Not a lot of people are using it.' So we'll teach them how to post stuff that creates 'talkability' – that starts a conversation with their people. If you've got a leader or a director who can just go and post something that caught his or her eye over the weekend – maybe a newspaper article or a TV show – that's the kind of thing that will get it all rolling.

It's about the leaders and directors taking the initiative in some of those activities. And it doesn't need to be a strain on their time, because all they need to do is post one question or comment and ask people to give their views, and initiate that two-way conversation. We're getting better at that, and we now have some directors who are fantastic – and others who are improving all the time!

Annabel: When employees do give their feedback and comment on what a director or leader has written, how well do you think your organization acts on that feedback?

Lindsey: It depends what feedback we're working with. With the annual employee survey, for example, it takes about a month to get the results and feedback through. And then when we do get the feedback, the ideal is that the leader of the team sits down and builds an action plan – then works on it throughout the year, involving his or her team.

The annual survey responses are broken down into teams, so that you know how your people are thinking and feeling as a group. You also know what areas you need to work on during the year ahead, in order to address insights from the survey. So by the time the next one comes up, hopefully those questions have been addressed because you've actually worked through your action plans to make sure that happens.

Unfortunately, that isn't always the case. It might happen in a very few teams, but I think everyone will have good intentions immediately after the survey, and the plans are drawn up. Then time elapses and other priorities arise. A month before the next annual survey is due to go out, everyone gets out their action plans and remembers that they were supposed to deliver the X, Y and Z. They revisit the survey in a rush to try to deliver, so that they can say they've done it by the time the next one comes around. That's really not the way to do it!

However, there are other kinds of feedback such as our Yammer debates. We have quite a few Q and As on this platform. A good example would be that more often than not our chairman will do a Yammer debate with employees around our quarterly results. Several days beforehand, the chairman will post some really open questions and this leads to lots of people online responding to those questions. We always say that if we can't give an immediate response, we will do so within a given timeframe. Then, when the chairman is online he will often spend a few hours responding directly to people.

Annabel: Is it anonymous or do people post their names?

Lindsey: We encourage people to leave their names in the interests of transparency, so it is very open, although it took a little while for people to adopt that openness – because I think they do like to say something but stay anonymous.

The whole Yammer trend does have its limitations. It doesn't do everything that we want it to do. But it is a network, a platform that is working well within Telefónica. It's taken a while to get there but I think we now have about 80,000 employees who are part of the global Yammer network.

The great thing is that we have an excellent chairman. He is a real people person. So he knows the value of talking to people, getting their views. We are lucky he will take the time out of his busy schedule to take part in the debates, and he'll respond to as many people as possible. Even after the debate is finished – and they last about an hour and a half – he will continue to pick up conversations, responding over the course of the week to those he hasn't had the time to answer. And the great thing is that more and more of our leaders are adopting that kind of approach.

Another area where we have an open opportunity for employees is on our intranet. Our UK intranet is a good example of giving employees the opportunity to respond to news and stories. They will often leave comments, and it's where IC can go and view the feedback and get people's insights into various things that are going on.

Town halls are also always very good and very vocal – and they work extremely well in our UK business. We also hold open forums with directors. For example, here in our London office, we have a director who comes over from Madrid. He's engaged and interested in the people who are based in this building. He hosts very informal forums. Everyone sits on beanbags and he will just talk without slides or anything like that for about 10 minutes, and then open it up to Q and A. It gives people the opportunity to ask questions. Once someone asks that first question, it opens up the flood-gates. They get braver. And I like to think that most of our directors will answer those questions as openly and honestly as they can at the time.

All in all, you can see we have quite a few channels – and that really speaks to our openness, and how we invite people to say what they want to say.

Life of privilege

This seemed like a good moment to get personal with Lindsey. She had spoken a lot about the value of IC to the business and its increasingly strategic status in the higher levels of the organization. But we were intrigued to find out what kind of impact nearly two decades of inhabiting the gradually evolving world of IC has had on her personally – and what it has brought her in terms of satisfaction and inspiration. As with so many of our subjects, the answer turned out to be surprisingly humble.

As an IC professional, she explained, you are simply in a very lucky and privileged position – and if you take the opportunity, you will benefit from meeting different people from all walks of the business. Specializing in IC allows you to behave like a butterfly, never focused on one specific area. One day you're engaged with HR, the next with marketing or innovation teams. Then the Big Data guys come calling, or sales, and different worlds of experiences open up on a daily basis. For Lindsey, that variety is the stuff of IC life. It's consistently engaging, and it gives her the chance to be involved in lots of the creative and fun aspects of working at Telefónica.

The other thing that comes with the territory is that you never know what each day will bring. The idea of having a fixed schedule that maps out your day so that you know precisely what you're going to be doing will never really work. Invariably your phone will ring, or someone will come in and say, 'Hi, I've got campaign X coming up. I'm going to launch it next week and I really need your help. Have you got some ideas for any branding elements and imagery? And basically, can you tell us what we need to do?'

As she told us earlier, it's not just about writing the content. You get involved in every aspect of a campaign, from intranet copy to video and infographic production. There is a huge range of channels, and what you realize is that when you meet a team who need your help – and you're able to give them so many different ideas about how they can get their message across – those are the moments when your role as an IC specialist really gels.

Smell the roses

Taking a step back and considering the sheer variety of activities that now come under the IC umbrella is a salutary moment. But for Lindsey, the overriding realization is that interaction with so many different people and teams, and participation in such a diverse range of activities and campaigns, also affords you the possibility to have loads of fun along the way. If someone comes to you and announces that he or she wants to do an event, you can instantly get into gear, brainstorming ideas, thinking outside the box and bringing something different to the table. And that helps to build your reputation as someone who can step in and help. Referrals and recommendations keep the IC network in a constant state of development – and its diversity, according to Lindsey, can be phenomenal. These are the fruits of a career in internal communications.

Annabel: What advice would you give to an up-and-coming internal communicator, perhaps someone studying communications – and what kind of skills do they need?

Lindsey: Embrace it because it offers so many opportunities. There are so many different ways that you can go. You could focus on events, or online and social media. Embrace that variety. In terms of skills, I think you need to be open and honest. You need to be a really good listener because you must understand the requirements of what people are asking you. You can't just go off at a tangent. You need to be able to understand their vision and what your internal customer wants from you. That's a key skill. Being open and honest is critical as well. People might come to you with an idea, and sometimes you have to be very direct as an internal communicator. That is not always easy!

Another skill is knowing your audience and stakeholders. It's really important. Because if you want something to work, you need to get the right stakeholders to the table at the very beginning. When you're new to the business, one of the first things to do is draw a map: find out as much as you can about the organization, its strategy, and who your key stakeholders are. Who are the people you need to get out there and meet, or who might come to you for your advice? Who are the people that can make things happen!

Annabel: How does your organization keep sight of corporate purpose during periods of change?

Lindsey: We have 125,000 employees spread across 21 different countries. There are always big changes going on in the company as a result of re-organizations, mergers and acquisitions, launches of new products into the market. When these big transitional pieces happen, the key thing that we try to be is very open-minded with our employees and always offer an open platform where they can share their concerns. We tend to ramp up things like town halls and informal forums, where people have the face-to-face opportunity to ask about what's going to happen in the company – and to get direct responses. That's where Yammer comes in, providing a place for open debate about transitional periods and organizational changes.

But it's also about that commitment to employees, and saying upfront: 'We're going through a period of transition and we appreciate and realize that this can be unsettling for you.' In the past when we've had big changes, we've made a commitment to communicate every fortnight with employees, whether there's anything to say or not: a promise to keep them updated. We'll also post a formalized Q and A on the intranet, which we'll keep updating to ensure the messages are clear and consistent. It's about keeping the communication channels open.

A very good example occurred last year, when there was a proposed sale of our UK business to Hutchinson. During that whole period, it was unsettling for our employees. So there was a big communications push around constantly keeping them up to speed with what was happening through open forums, CEO messages and Yammer debates, and a dedicated intranet timeline that was always up to date. The UK team commissioned special videos to take people through the different stages of the proposed sale so people had a better understanding in the event that the company was sold. Every effort was made to ensure they understood all the different jargon.

Again, it's about being really open, trying to keep our channels open and making that commitment to employees that we will update them, regardless of whether there's any news or not.

Shock tactics

As a global business with a strong UK presence, Telefónica surely kept a close eye on the implications of the EU Referendum in June 2016. We wondered, in particular, how the messaging on what turned out to be a tumultuous result was handled internally.

Lindsey explained that, typically, in cases where wider political influences are likely to impact on the organization, IC takes the lead from the external comms team. Any official comment or press release would be shared before publication, and adapted internally. In the case of Brexit, this was complemented by an intranet Q and A that interpreted and set out the possibilities of the outcome as discussed by reputable external media, reinforcing the sense that the business was keeping abreast of events rather than just waiting for something to happen. Given the referendum result and the prolonged fall-out of uncertainty, we were curious about the additional challenges this might have created for IC in a business with an international workforce. Lindsey said that, not surprisingly, the sense of shock was widespread – and the need to 'watch this space' and endure a prolonged wait for answers certainly did not help. What it did underline was the value of being surrounded by a well-connected, multi-skilled team with the ability to hold a steady course.

No one is an island

You can't do everything on your own, Lindsey reminded us, however experienced you are. If you have a good cross-section of people who enjoy internal communications as much as you do – and who are really good at it because they understand its importance and the value it brings to the business – you are in a strong position to roll with the punches that will come at you, internally and externally.

It was interesting to learn – and another example of the extent to which IC is now part of the fabric and language of the business – how Lindsey often hears about teams being set up in which someone is given responsibility for internal communications, as if anyone can just step up and do it without any previous form, background or relevant experience. Her response to that is that actually, no, they can't. You wouldn't make such a presumption in any other part of the business. Being good at IC takes the right mindset. An internal comms person, she told us, has to be outgoing, able to connect with everyone involved in the campaign, and accepting of constructive criticism. Getting your leaders involved in IC when they don't really want to know can be hard. And it's far from the case that anyone can do it.

Managing and measuring employee engagement

02

Experience in a competitive industry sector with traditionally high levels of staff turnover

SUZIE WELCH, People Director, PizzaExpress

JO HARVEY, Engagement and Communications Manager, PizzaExpress

Internal communications is a luxury discipline. The board believes in its value but, at the end of the day, it remains a good thing to have rather than an essential. That's the telling assessment of Jo Harvey, Engagement and Communications Manager at PizzaExpress, a business in which IC is clearly rising up the agenda and increasingly perceived as a key engagement tool. When Jo took our Pulse Check™, the results were intriguing. They revealed the underlying tension between the vision of a company that's going global, fast, and the challenge of interpreting and channelling the all-important feedback and contributions of employees into that vision.

The desire to achieve this is obvious – in Jo's vivid descriptions of the ways in which rapid progress is being made, and in her uncompromising passion for driving engagement. The opportunity to hear, at first hand, how this tension is helping to define and deliver the benefits of an enlightened IC strategy in the dynamic culture of an instantly recognizable restaurant chain promised some unique insights into the hows and whys of success.

At PizzaExpress, HR is called the 'People Team'. The role of Engagement and Comms reports directly to the People Director – her voice on the board. The business is structured around a geographical hierarchy: regions, areas and 463 (and rising) restaurant locations. The role of Engagement and Comms Manager is to lead the engagement agenda with 11,500 employees across these locations, most of whom – waiters, cleaners, pizzaiolos, managers – are restaurant-based. Making sure they are all aware of the latest business news and events, and constantly working on how the company builds retention throughout the business are two major areas of focus; reaching them is always a challenge, bearing in mind that they are working with customers rather than sitting in front of a computer all day waiting for 'broadcasts'.

The solution is to cascade messages from the top down through the hierarchy of the business. But Jo is clear that the channels also need to be in place for messages coming in the other direction, so that the challenges faced by operators on the front line are heard loud and clear by restaurant support people, who can then put strategies in place to help solve them. Human contact is an essential aspect of the cascade approach at regional and area levels: frequent face-to-face meetings between restaurant managers, area managers and operations managers. This is the preferred method for 'big' messages and internal campaigns, backed up with the intranet and e-mail.

Annabel: How would you say IC is perceived as a profession today?

Suzie: It's changed beyond recognition in the past three to five years. It's now seen as one of the distinguishing factors of a good business, because keeping employees engaged and aware of the context behind news and events is more and more important.

Annabel: Do you think that one of the reasons why a board can still see IC as a luxury is because they need the business equation to be proved to them?

Suzie: Yes, because the operational challenges can outweigh the people priorities. Sometimes things need to be put into place quickly and communication can be disregarded. There is a constant challenge to ensure that we work hard to not make decisions at the cost of the engagement but sometimes it isn't possible or we just get it wrong.

Annabel: Can you elaborate on how the company has kept focus on its purpose during change?

Suzie: The business is 50 years old and has seen so much change in that time. We are not the business we were; just our sheer size challenges how we maintain a view of our direction and keep the message consistent and relevant for everyone, both in the UK and across the world. More recently, the speed of change has increased and therefore it becomes challenging to keep everyone up to date with where we are. People can only remember so much.

Having said that, it is clear that our purpose hasn't changed in all that time: when you strip it back we serve pizza – really good pizza. Quality pizza and enjoyable experiences have always been at the heart of what we do. However, we can have a lot of new people join us every year so helping them to connect to our purpose and then deliver it means it is key to have strong IC channels.

Annabel: How has this impacted IC messaging to your team?

Jo: It's always been the priority to make sure that our people are the first to know. Comms plans are always worked out to make sure the right people learn first. They follow quite a strict process, determining who gets told face-to-face or by phone. Then it's a matter of filtering it down the organization. There are always face-to-face communications to back up any big piece of news, whether it's through a video conference, a conference call or a meeting where everyone gets together. Communications are always based on our strategic priorities and what are we trying to achieve. That has never changed. It's always been reinforced; that's the message.

Annabel: Can you say what works well by doing it in that way? And what hasn't worked quite so well?

Jo: What's worked well is that no one's had their nose put out of joint! Egos exist. People don't want to feel like they're the last to know. So, that side of things has worked really, really well. What hasn't worked so well is feeding the thoughts, feelings and emotions of people back up the chain – how you can capture that sense of nervousness or uncertainty created by change, and how that then is reflected in the business.

The retention challenge

Retention is one of the biggest challenges in the restaurant industry. How do you successfully recruit, train and retain a strong workforce in the face of stiff competition, tight margins, shifting employment patterns and a climate in which migratory labour – the lifeblood of the catering and hospitality sector – is under scrutiny as never before? Given the youthful profile of employees in the industry, it has been one of the earliest beneficiaries of the advent of the millennial worker. It has also proved a febrile testing ground for strategies to identify and hold on to the best of them, bringing as they do an acute sense of consumer brand ownership in harness with some clearly defined job and career expectations. Before we spoke, Jo had signposted the role of brand proposition in recruitment and retention in our Pulse Check™ so we were not surprised that it is being woven into PizzaExpress's people strategy with urgency and commitment.

An employee app, giving people instant access to rotas and payslips, providing newsfeeds in formats they are used to – all these innovations have been successful, and even exceeded Jo's anticipation. But there are other factors to accommodate, not least the changing nature and skill sets of school-leavers, and the impact of changing pay rates for people up to the age of 21, and then 25. Ensuring equality, openness and transparency on pay parity has been among the many things requiring a big focus.

Annabel: If you had a blank canvas and you could treat millennials in the way you think they need to be treated, what other initiatives would you put in place?

Jo: Training. I would put all the money in the world into it. Millennials want stuff instantly but I think it's a misconception that they want something for nothing. They do want to be able to develop and grow, and be passionate about something. They need to be given that opportunity. Sometimes you have to work a bit harder to reach them, but once you've got them on board, I think they're loyal.

Annabel: Purpose and what the company stands for beyond them getting their pay cheque and having a stimulating work environment – do you think that's important to them?

Jo: Yes, definitely. I know from some of the work we've been doing that pay is definitely not the be all and end all. They want to work for a company that's seen to be doing good. They want to be able to tell their mates that they work somewhere cool. Giving back something is important to millennials.

Suzie: Last year, as a business we decided to partner with a charity. Rather than the board pick the charity, we shortlisted four and then asked our teams to vote for the one that they wanted to support. This was then announced as one of the key messages at our conference. From there it has been about enabling the teams to support in the way they want to. To kick off all of this activity we held a fundraising week where we challenged each restaurant to raise some money. The teams didn't just achieve the target: they smashed it. Much of this we believe was down to the role that the team played in the whole process, part of the decision making not just being asked to deliver. Even now they continue to raise money and own driving the partnership forward.

Annabel: Do you see any key trends emerging?

Jo: I think it's all going to become digitalized and app-based. Going forward, it's just the best way of reaching people.

Annabel: How will that work with the more mature elements of your workforce? Are they as comfortable with the apps as you've found millennials to be?

Jo: I can only recall five employees so far who've not wanted our app. In those instances, I'm not too worried because they're not missing any information that isn't also going to be cascaded to our other traditional channels. We're never going to get rid of those cascade channels, ever. So, they will just hear things in the normal way. Also, the more people that are getting news through the app, the more they're sharing it with colleagues. Employees are hearing about the app from the others and saying, 'Why haven't I got it?' And then they're chasing me to get it.

Frustrated ambitions

One area in which high staff turnover has had a particular impact is ongoing engagement. This remains a challenge for any restaurant business dependent on a relatively fluid workforce. The annual employee engagement survey, with its once-a-year dataset, is markedly less effective at capturing the trends and flows of the staff zeitgeist, which can turn on a sixpence and leave a business playing catch-up with the very people who should be its greatest brand champions. Quite simply, as Jo told us in her Pulse Check™, an organization like PizzaExpress has too high a turnover to base an engagement score on a one-off survey. Twelve months is too long to wait for the next set of data, and it is impossible to achieve any consistent measurement. Instead, there should be a blended approach with two-way comms for best engagement – targeting specific groups with specific questions, and getting to the heart of what it is that matters to people.

Jo readily admitted that this has been a struggle to get going with any traction: partly because of the volume of activity within the business, but also because of her own nervousness. If the company is going to ask its people important questions, she wants to be able to demonstrate that the data is going somewhere, and that it will lead to the implementation of changes and responses. The day-to-day job of engagement does not always leave room for the innovation she would like! Indeed, if anything it is becoming more overwhelming. That is a sentiment we can fully sympathize with – an all-too-familiar scenario. At the same time, we were hugely encouraged by Jo's vision for greater engagement, which surely raises the bar for any business that is serious about a meaningful and integrated IC strategy, however impeded its trajectory might be by daily practicalities. Onwards and upwards, we say. But first, how about the elusive evidence that could help persuade the board to free IC from its luxury tag and put it centre stage?

Annabel: How do you measure the impact of IC?

Jo: Good question! We measure it in a very flat way in terms of the number of people who opened an e-mail, viewed a video, or commented on an intranet article. All of that gives us metrics. But other than that the actual impact of IC is not measured.

Annabel: Again, if you could wave your magic wand, what would you want to implement there?

Suzie: A mix of things really. We want to be able to measure whether people have read information and whether they understand it, but really we want to understand the impact of what we have done. Surveys can always give us that quick read of the impact but having a regular process of talking to the teams and then acting on their feedback is most important; the ability to be able to explore further and build on what we have done.

Annabel: Once you've got that data in through technology or face-to-face, do you believe PizzaExpress and/or your team are good at acting on employee feedback?

Suzie: I think we are getting better – it takes real focus and energy. You have to be able to dissect the key elements and utilize them to take action. We are working hard to put this on regular agendas, using the survey feedback to start the conversation, backed up by our face-to-face feedback and then working through what this means and what is that action we would like to take. Early days, but we are moving forward each month.

The key is not to go into overdrive and change the world/react to every piece of feedback – few and impactful is key: to really deliver a strong two-way communication culture, where our teams feel like they can reach the people they need to, to feed back, and we can touch every employee in the right way with key messages. It can become easy to drive everything through one channel that you see as successful but the challenge for IC is to keep this moving and not rely on one way; a blend of technology and human contact but always with a story to tell.

The long game

This was a poignant moment in our conversation – the point at which Jo's frustrations with the restrictions and impediments unwittingly imposed on IC by operating decisions and strategies seemed to collide with her passion for meeting the challenges of engagement. Innovation often stems from this conflict – again, a very recognizable scenario for so many IC practitioners. Yet it can be a long game, and it requires precisely the vision and commitment that IC practitioners like Jo bring to the business. Breaking the vicious circle requires a change in attitudes across the business – and crucially, in the boardroom.

Jo told us her passion for IC is rooted in the scope it offers for connecting with people: finding out why they get out of bed in the morning and come to work, and the chain of events that leads to giving a customer the most positive experience. She would prefer to reference a virtuous circle – happy team, happy customer – founded on nice stories and good news. Asking her about the downside of her role unleashed a familiar ghoul: internal politics and the need to try to please too many people when all that should really matter is the audience for her message, and what they get out of it. She has, however, learnt the value of diplomacy: a requisite gift for the IC practitioner. These days, with her experience in conflict resolution, Jo thinks she could easily work for the UN. We don't doubt it for a second.

Annabel: Can you describe the sort of skills you think you need to be a great advocate for IC?

Jo: Influencing skills are critical. The ability to make stuff happen, because normally in IC you work by yourself or in a very small team. You have to be able to come up with the ideas and stick to them. You also have to be good at building relationships because you need to be the go-to person, the central person in the organization that people come to.

Annabel: If you were advising someone in a new role, how would you help them become that go-to person?

Jo: Treat your people like your stakeholders or customers. When I was on the other side of the fence – I used to work on the front line with customers in a sales role – I would do exactly the same. I think of our restaurant managers as my customers: what have I got to do to make the right thing happen for them? How do they need it to happen? You build up a reputation for being a useful person, but you have got to be able to see ideas through and remember the little things. Also, always put faces to names and always bring the story-telling element into IC because that's the bit people remember. Then they'll remember that it came from you, and that you did good stuff.

Annabel: What are your top three tips for anyone working in IC today?

Jo: Listen. Know your audience. And don't assume anything!

Annabel: Where do you see IC in five years' time?

Jo: The role is becoming more important than previously. I can only judge it on my experience but I definitely see it changing more from internal communications to engagement. And therefore its focus is moving towards retention and the employee proposition.

When Jo drew a strong parallel between internal and external communications, it occurred to us that this is often the missing link in any corporate comms strategy. Where is the line actually drawn between the two? Indeed, just because they have traditionally been treated as separate disciplines, should there be a line at all? As Jo told us, when she was recruited into the comms team she had what she calls a 'dotted line' to the people. Now that she is part of the people team, she has a dotted line to external comms. She is, she says, 'sitting in the middle'. From the outside, it is almost as though she is biding her time until formal integration becomes part of the strategy. She offered Starbucks in the United States as an example of this already happening. Starbucks partners (team members) have a 'brilliant' Twitter feed, which is well-run and a great example of where internal and external comms have merged.

External comms can be too preoccupied with brand reputation and hiding the kinds of things employees might talk about on social media. But actually, if organizations want to change people's brand perceptions, what they really need to do is get their employees to become brand ambassadors – something which can't happen without a good IC function. Jo's belief that external comms simply can't operate without IC rang a loud bell for us. We think it could be about time to cross that particular line and erase it altogether.

Annabel: What are your inspirations? Do you have time beyond the day job to attend events, read books or follow any particular feeds?

Jo: I love Buzzfeed! But my inspirations are more people rather than events and things like that. I keep an eye on what people like Danny Meyer are doing. (Meyer is the New York restaurateur and CEO of the Union Square Hospitality Group, an acclaimed innovator who recently opened one of the sector's biggest cans of worms by banning tipping in his restaurants.) When those 'Best Companies to Work For' lists come out (*Fortune* and *The Sunday Times* both publish their own), I take a look and see who's there. I always keep an eye on what some of our competitors are doing. I don't tend to go to the events with other people because I think every organization is so incredibly different, and we have such specific needs here. It's probably quite bad of me. I should but I just don't have time!

I read a really good book the other week – *Quiet: The power of introverts in a world that can't stop talking* by Susan Cain. She says that where extroverts get so much focus and attention, there are plenty of introverts doing amazing work. You just don't necessarily hear their voices because they aren't the loudest. So the book explores how you might get the most out of that.

Shifts in perception

At some point in our interviews, all our subjects identified a shift in the way IC is being perceived and exploited by their organizations. That seems like good news. It is, after all, one of the main reasons that we felt the time had come for a book like this. However, Jo's combination of enthusiasm for the possibilities of an expanding strategic remit for IC, occasionally tempered by her real-world observations about the hindrance that can come from established hierarchies and entrenched attitudes, struck a particularly resonant chord with us. She is optimistic that change will come, and that the facilitating tools will continue to emerge and support it. Good IC demands a central role today – and will claim a bigger one in the future. If anybody wants to launch something new within an organization, the best strategy and platform in the world won't help if you can't cut through to the people who will actually be delivering it. IC deserves its higher prominence today – but tomorrow, says Jo, practitioners are going to change the world.

Grant Thornton 03

How the evolution of an authentic internal voice is helping to drive essential change in an increasingly turbulent and challenging climate for business leaders

NORMAN PICKAVANCE

Leader of the Brand, Innovation & Sustainability Agenda,

Grant Thornton

There are comms evangelists with a passion for and belief in the value of transparency. And then there is Norman Pickavance who, as quickly became clear during our conversation, takes that commitment to a whole new level. Norman has spent three decades in influential comms roles in the public and private sectors, including a variety of HR directorships at Perot, ICL, Northern Foods, Marconi and Morrisons. He has also spent a year and a half as a non-executive director at HM Revenue & Customs, advising the board on a major organizational, cultural and leadership change that affected more than 60,000 employees. With this pedigree, he has perhaps found his natural home as Leader of the Brand, Innovation & Sustainability Agenda at Grant Thornton, the global business adviser and accounting organization focused on helping dynamic companies to unlock their growth potential.

Norman's wisdom

In 2014, Norman published *The Reconnected Leader,* a book that pinpoints the huge corporate renewal challenges for many organizations in a business world facing unprecedented national and global upheaval, at a time when people's trust in leaders is at an all-time low. His proposition is that those leaders must effectively reinvent themselves as visionary communicators who can convey messages and strategies in terms that are at once inspirational and realistic. The age of shiny corporate-speak has been superseded by expectations of honest and open communications. We have lost any tolerance for obscure and convoluted messaging. The best comms practitioners have grasped this, and now focus on engagement through straight-talking and clearly signposted narratives. It rapidly dawned on us that this shift informs his best practice advocacy at every level, and he wasted no time in identifying what he sees as a major tension at the heart of IC.

Imogen: How do you believe internal communications is perceived today?

Norman: To my mind, today, internal communications is in two distinct and different places. The first is that it acts as a mouthpiece to ensure people get the message. People want to hear what companies have to say; they want new information – but innately, they don't trust it when it is shared. Why is that? Partly because IC has become a lot slicker and is almost *too* polished. What a CEO says internally may not be the same as what is reported externally. And people aren't daft. If the two sets of messages don't tally up, they won't believe you. It's as simple as that.

The second point is that we live in a complicated world with complex businesses. While people want transparency and for information to be inclusive, they reject the traditional cascade approach. We are moving towards more openness but I'm not sure we are there yet.

There is a need for IC expertise in terms of how you make the internal voice of a company 'authentic'. At Grant Thornton, the firm decided to review its business strategy down to the very foundations of its core business. This exercise alone threw up 19 goals for the company to achieve to take it forward. Clearly, this is too many! So what did we do? Well, rather than simply announce our findings to the wider population, we began by sharing the 19 goals with our partnership population. Then we shared the goals with the wider business so that everyone had an opportunity to contribute.

Some very interesting results came out of this. A 'sharing ideas' process evolved that enabled the firm to engage with 2,500 of its employees, online or face-to-face, through a workshop format. These workshops focused on asking people what they thought of the strategy, the goals, and what other ideas should be considered. All of this feedback was fed into the next iteration of the firm's strategy and then went back to the partnership population, who could provide their final comments and observations. In short, we effected a comprehensive dialogue with our people. In return, we collected a deeper perspective on the direction they felt we should be taking as a business.

The whole process was very interactive and inclusive. Here's an example: as part of the workshop format, we would set up a room with posters on the walls capturing the ideas and innovations, and then ask people to comment. They could take their time and reflect on their responses, and we ended up with a rich and varied panorama of ideas, many of them new.

We used a lot of this feedback to inform our strategic review, which we have since shared both internally and externally. It also led to the creation of the 'Shared enterprise', which hosts Grant Thornton's collective thinking on what a shared enterprise looks like, how can we create it, how we enable a greater sense of ownership across the firm, and how we can get people to act more responsibly.

Connected vision

Norman's description of a thorough and comprehensive engagement process, which delivered powerful information to incorporate in the business's strategy for change, should give any IC practitioner in a similar position considerable food for thought. At no point did he suggest it was easy, but it was obviously the result of a very considered assessment of the impact of new technology on communication at every level in our lives, how this continues to drive expectations of engagement in new directions – and how IC in particular can harness the benefits of these changes, rather than remain trapped in reactive limbo. As he told us, if you buy the vision of a connected world and the seismic number of digital interactions that are taking place across the planet, you will hardly be surprised at how easy it is for people in power to misread the views of their population. In these interesting times, such home truths are raining down on governments and politicians – and business leaders are increasingly subject to similar wake-up calls, from shareholders, employees, and broader social and political influences.

Norman suggests that better connectivity is one answer: if we connect different groups together and encourage them to come up with solutions to life's bigger challenges, we may discover new and innovative ways to solve problems, rather than relying on previously trusted methods that may be tainted with suspicion or failure. Just because you've always done something one way, and it is generally seen as the norm, it isn't necessarily the right way. Norman believes that organizations need to take in a wider eco-system, and accept that they have to be a 'multi-connected' node, to really understand what their people think. It's a powerful concept, and he acknowledged that it requires a significant amount of commitment to bring it to life.

More and more businesses today find themselves disconnected at a corporate and individual level. Norman says this is happening for a host of reasons; the key is to keep trying to understand and appreciate how many aspects of business life are humanized and depend on open communication. He thinks this is especially difficult for men right now – although this can change with the help of legislation and the rise of flexible working; traditionally, they are less burdened with everyday communications, even if they are family men. It's too easy for them to come to work and just focus on the job. After a while, if you fall into that kind of rhythm, you start looking at the world through a distorted lens, and this makes you lose sight of things. The more you lose sight of, the more disconnected you become – and at a leadership level, Norman says, this can have a significant impact. When leadership becomes disconnected, it usually boils down to a loss of trust with your population. And that is hard to build back up.

Imogen: How does IC get played out as part of your corporate purpose?

Norman: This is a fascinating area of how a business defines itself and forces the question – what is our purpose beyond making money? Companies today have to be clear about how they are creating value for society. Once you are clear about how you are doing that, then you can be clear about your purpose. At Grant Thornton, this impacts on three core areas of our business:

1 *Financial sector* – we work with a range of clients helping them to foster assurance that what people are doing is true – for example, the International Monetary Fund (IMF) and Greece, our remediation work at Barclays, and working with RBS as a bank facing a significant challenge of public perception.

2 *Sustainability* – we work with mid-sized businesses (usually those that are family-owned), and help them identify ways to grow sustainably. This is not a short-term initiative or just about profit extraction. This work is defined by its very purpose and long-term trajectory.

3 *Public sector* – 40 per cent of the audits Grant Thornton carries out are in the public sector and these are instrumental in helping to create businesses where people can thrive. What we're especially interested in is understanding what makes for a vibrant economy; such audits are an essential part of this.

The 'Vibrant economy' has become a significant piece of work for the firm and will form a core component of our overall communications strategy going forward. We're aiming to bring this to life by engaging markets and people in terms of what a 'Vibrant economy' means for them.

Grant Thornton has been running a series of city enquiries across the country. For example, in Sheffield we brought together

200 leaders. The discussions were facilitated by us and focused on what Sheffield needs to do to become a vibrant economy. This session alone generated 600 new ideas.

To my mind, if you have a diversity of views that is engaging Grant Thornton people, clients and prospects across the world, it gives you an outside/in approach. This helps to reposition the brand and encourage our people to think about their role within the firm in a different way. We want to directly engage people in real conversations because we believe they deliver greater value and help us move the business forward. It's not just about the numbers. It's about tapping into your intellectual capital and provoking new ideas and approaches that allow you to innovate.

Our next enquiry is about the future of health, and will be run in Manchester. It will look specifically at how can we use dynamic insight to co-design solutions to improve our health services. Grant Thornton's approach with these enquiries is to take a less corporate, humbler approach so that we have everyone working together to come up with better answers. We think this makes us a better business to work for and is progressive.

We want to continually create a sense of purpose across our firm. There is an enormous difference between a 'collaboration and creation' and a 'command and control' modus operandi. The more we can veer towards collaboration and creation, the better our ideas will be and, I would suggest, the more engaged our people will be.

Conversation starters

We wanted to probe a little deeper into how this is influencing IC practice within Grant Thornton and how, in turn, IC practice manifests itself across the business. Again, Norman's characteristic mix of plain speaking and evocative story-telling enlivened his response. Grant Thornton is succeeding, he said, by 'sticking to the knitting'. This means an emphasis on internal, interactive and highly discursive events such as town hall meetings, which aim to provide everyone with business updates. They are deliberately designed to start conversations across the organization, and to demonstrate the firm's commitment to a listen-and-participate approach to employee engagement, rather than the traditional and increasingly out-of-date IC practice of simply 'telling' people what's going on.

Norman emphasized Grant Thornton's commitment to being a highly relational firm, in which the cultural fit is all-important. Kindness is valued enormously, he said. When key decisions are made, a great deal of thought is put into how people are impacted. Of course there are times when this might slow down the business – but Norman can't recall a single example when the outcome failed to justify the means. In essence, he told us, it amounts to taking a very human approach, demonstrating that what the business wants above everything else is a genuine conversation with its employees. That translates into taking a positive interest in its staff as people, and in their family lives and priorities – and making that interest a natural element of any meeting.

He also sets a lot of store by humour. Norman believes that as human beings we are generally well intentioned. But we can also be messy, sometimes, and there has to be a degree of tolerance and acceptance so that people feel they can be themselves. To err is human, he reassured us. And it's a really important aspect of how we learn. Millennials, perhaps, don't always have a reputation for such a measured and sympathetic response to human frailty – but Norman clearly feels their influence on IC is, and will continue to be, positive in many different ways.

Imogen: How are you managing the impact of millennials in the workplace?

Norman: We have a lot of millennials working for us and all of them are looking for purpose and meaning in the workplace. Take a look at the Ashridge report which was carried out in 2014 (*The Millennial Compass: Truths about the 30-and-under generation in the workplace*, for MSL Group). It consisted of a review of what millennials think – and the upshot is it all comes down to wanting to make a difference to the world around them. We have other employees in the firm who think differently and are more focused on the short term and how much their bonus will be. But there's so much more to work than that. Millennials bring a refreshing perspective to why we work and that is something we are actively embracing as a firm.

Imogen: How are increased regulation and transparency impacting you as a company?

Norman: No amount of compliance or regulation will make people do the right thing. You can spend a fortune on it but it still won't stop bad things happening. Grant Thornton is regulated by the Financial Conduct Authority as you would expect. Our focus is how we can get our clients to behave with trust and integrity, and how will this help us create sustainable growth. There is no simple answer. If we have a client who is in choppy waters, we need to look at how we get involved and help them act with integrity. When you enter into this part of the process, judgement and dialogue are key. The decisions made have to stand up to scrutiny. All of this becomes an ongoing discourse. What does that mean in practice? Well, that we need to have a conversation and explain ourselves with maturity. However, these scenarios are never black and white.

It's really important to move away from immediate judgements and see the situation in balance. You shouldn't beat a business up to get it to behave in an honest way. It's a longer process than that. Equally, it's important to understand how corporate image works. Corporate social responsibility (CSR), for example, is the presentation of a perfect picture. CSR doesn't allow you to have any flaws as a company. So the picture isn't realistic. The amount of money that businesses spend on augmenting their image today is excessive and unlikely to decrease in the immediate future. Sadly, society isn't mature enough just yet to have the right kind of conversation when something goes wrong, and not to rush to judgement over it.

Imogen: Do you believe the annual engagement survey is dead?

Norman: I think people have lost faith in its original purpose, and whether the survey can actually fix the issue or issues it might raise. The challenge with any type of survey is that it needs to answer at least two key questions: 1) Does it move the agenda forward? 2) Does it address the real issues people are talking about?

We might know what the big issues are: that the quality of working relationships is a perennial issue, for example, but what we actually need to be finding out is what's going on in the world of the employee. Appreciating and understanding how busy managers are is pivotal. This notion of command and control doesn't really work. The reality is that managers are passing information on, but they don't really know themselves what's going on. They have no context. And our job, as senior leaders, is to help and support them in their roles so they can manage their responsibilities a lot more easily.

There are processes and habits we're changing in our business on the back of deeper conversations. Let me give you an example of this: we have quite a traditional process for winning new work, which comprises a long list of potential new clients – a wish-list if you like. What we have done recently is to prioritize a group of these targets, and agree a list of, say, 20 names. The process is now very structured and highly inclusive. Everyone is committed to it and it is completely transparent. As a result, people keep coming up with ideas on how to improve their world and make this part of their roles easier for them to manage.

Another example of changing the way we do things was to stop sending out 'CEO Updates'. This was simply a broadcast tool for us; we just sent information out but provided no answers. Our leadership team recently group-identified six areas for us to focus on as a business, and one of these is how can accelerate the number of internal promotions. This is a topic that resonates strongly across our teams. It also links to our goal of creating a shared enterprise, whereby everyone works together to solve a challenge or issue in the firm. What that means is that we are all prepared to go through the frustrations of a given process and collaborate on the solutions.

Is it working?

So far in our conversation, Norman had been clear about the value of new processes to enable transparency and generate meaningful internal dialogue. But as with all our interview subjects, he also acknowledged that the ability to measure the outcome is the thing that, probably above all else, justifies the role of IC in the business.

Quite simply, as an IC practitioner, you need to know if what you're doing is working or not. There are important questions that the IC function, as well as the wider business, must be able to answer. On the strength of working more effectively as a team, are you winning more and different clients? What perception changes have there been to the business? Is your organization more attractive externally when it comes to hiring new people? Are you retaining more people?

Of course, once you have measured, you have to demonstrate that you've truly been listening by acting on the feedback. Norman told us that Grant Thornton's CEO has put seven questions to the business, which have morphed into seven areas of the business to progress. Hard and subjective measures such as brand image, customers the company is working with, and discussion groups, are used to chart that progress. There has been a huge shift in approach and attitude within the firm, from 'I am going to tell you what the answer is' to 'Let's work it out together'. Everyone is making mistakes together. The company has developed an innovative culture that equates to a willingness to experiment and encourages people to work in a world when there may not be an answer. Norman said this is based on constant experimentation. It isn't a question of passing or failing – it's now more of a question of whether the results are good or bad. In short, he said, Grant Thornton acts on the feedback, and very quickly and responsively too, because it is essential that people know they have been heard. They also need to know they can change things and have that 'Yes you can' mentality. It's a dynamic vision – and asking Norman to elaborate on some of the challenges that fuel it immediately revealed further layers of inspiration.

Imogen: What do you love the most about your role?

Norman: I thrive in a very creative space. We're living in interesting times and I find the broader economy is a stimulating place to be. I am drawn to how we can work differently in this space – and sometimes that can throw up some big questions. Leading major change can be personally very challenging, but I love it.

Imogen: What's the most important thing you have learnt along the way?

Norman: There are some things you have to do in business, but you have to live, eat and breathe the culture you exist in. Few leaders are tuned into this and yet in the broader world, people are taking responsibility. Sometimes this means coming up with different ways of doing things. Take the brewing industry. Today there are more craft breweries in the UK than anywhere else. All of them create and craft great beer while challenging the bigger brands at the same time. It's very positive to see this happening. Also, technology is enabling smaller, more flexible entities to build cultures that help them to compete and create in a more dynamic world. I think there will be lots of change in the next 25–30 years, with more and more people taking personal agency to make things happen.

One of the bigger challenges for larger companies is to be tuned into this and prepared to change the way they communicate. If you want to be part of a completely connected world, being comfortable with learning and experimenting within your own firm is key. At Grant Thornton, for instance, we might want to look at how we unplug from the grid. What would that look like in terms of power generation for our business? The disruption in the energy market is yet another example of how much business is changing.

Imogen: What are your top tips for someone seeking a career in internal communications?

Norman: First, recognize that the old silos which once defined roles in the organization are breaking down. Along with that comes the crossover between marketing, communications, people management, innovation, and so on. How you bring it all together is going to be really important – otherwise the world gets too complicated. If you look at what we do in IC, it's basically comms. But how you weave all these things together requires a much broader way of thinking and understanding. People who get that will also recognize that it's about how you include people in the process and bring them with you. I think it's very exciting.

Second, always take time to see what's going on outside your business. You need to work with people who get the importance of that, because they tend to bring a realistic perspective and context to what they do.

It is worth considering Norman's final tip in a little more detail. He would, he told us, commend a much-loved and inspirational William Wilberforce quote: 'You may choose to look the other way but you can never say again that you did not know.' Wilberforce was campaigning for the abolition of slavery in the 1800s, a movement close to Norman's heart. He is a vigorous campaigner for eradicating modern-day slavery, and for the pursuit of fair employment practices in the UK. Wilberforce's point that knowing something carries responsibility should resonate with leaders today. When you know the reality, you have a duty to communicate it clearly and honestly, and to act on that knowledge.

Trust and responsibility

What does this moving reference tell us about how we should be facing up to the responsibilities of IC, rather than simply delivering a corporate function? Norman closed our interview by observing that there is a dawning awareness that the corporate world inhabited by all IC practitioners is a little narrow. The penny dropped for him a long while ago, when he realized that there were many things he believed in that he wasn't actually doing anything about. So he started to get involved in the charity sector, and eventually ending up setting up a social enterprise that helped homeless people to get their lives back. The outside perception of organizations like Shelter, he told us, is that the solution they provide is getting homeless people somewhere to live. But that's the easy bit. It is actually about the reconstruction of a personal life.

Today, what interests Norman most is how we can help to rebuild trust between society and business. He is on a mission to discover if it is possible to create a genuinely connected organization and, if so, what it might look like. Clearly, he hopes that it will look something like Grant Thornton, once the process of change and evolution is complete. As a driver, it informs the company's economy agenda. The firm has just created a committee of 17 external commissioners from all walks of business, social and governmental life to investigate what people think a vibrant economy actually is. Norman is full of praise for their dynamism and finds working with them truly inspiring. On the strength of this, he is pulling together a narrative across all of the cities in the UK with the working title: 'In search of a vibrant Britain'. It will profile what's happening to make places like Sheffield and Manchester thriving economies. His greatest hope is that a new story will emerge from this rich process of engagement – a story that will energize and inspire.

There is a sense, he told us, that the principles and tenets that business has traditionally lived by are not working any more. This breeds uncertainty and mistrust for everyone in the comms chain. We all need compelling reasons to do things and a story that we can believe in. Norman's philosophy is startlingly simple: as an IC professional, you've got to try to generate ideas – then make them happen. The more we can encourage people to see something that they might not be happy with, and come up with an idea of how to make it better, the more the end result will astonish and surprise everyone. 'Just go and do it,' he offered as his parting shot. 'Don't wait for it to happen to you.' There is motivation there for all of us as we face up to the turbulent influences that are disrupting the business landscape today – and which present fresh challenges and opportunities for innovation, as we strive to help our people make sense of them.

BG Group

04

How your 'employer brand' is a dynamic and innovative power tool to unite a global workforce throughout corporate change

LAURA FERGUSON

People Engagement and Change, BG Group

So far, the interviews in this book have been strongly vision-focused. The need for a clear IC strategy, with the capacity to evolve and embrace change – particularly when it comes to the advent of new technologies and channels, and the arrival of millennials in the workplace – has been identified time and again by practitioners who between them have accumulated many decades of experience. But what about the actual skills you need to be a top-flight IC specialist in a complex, 21st-century business?

As Head of People Engagement and Change at BG Group, the British multinational oil and gas company recently taken over by Shell, Laura Ferguson has an insider's view of the make-up of an IC professional at the cutting edge – beginning with the value of learning and development. She strongly agrees with the 70:20:10 approach to personal development. The dominant element – the 70 per cent – comes from learning on the job, through day-to-day task performance, meeting and reflecting on regular challenges, and putting those lessons into practice. A further 20 per cent is acquired through social learning, with and through others, by being part of a team and contributing to its overall success. Only the final 10 per cent is realized through more formal processes such as courses and programmes.

An analytical mind lies at the heart of Laura's approach, together with a strong commercial instinct. If you understand the brand, which means understanding the business strategy, you can ask the essential probing questions. This business and commercial acumen isn't always seen as a prerequisite for IC but Laura was happy to share why she thinks it enables IC professionals to be more effective.

When we met, she was focusing on the skills, attributes and knowledge that contribute to excellence in IC. She is concerned that people go into IC with a strong journalistic zeal, armed with the soft skills of openness and curiosity, ready to question interpretations, acronyms and business impacts. Without a broader business and brand perspective some of their findings and conclusions may be lacking in depth, and may even alienate some audiences. She believes that by being able to have credible conversations at all levels of the organization, IC professionals earn their stripes. And this is particularly important when interacting with the middle management level, often the gateway – or blocker – in engaging and motivating the workforce. Identifying the problems to be solved, asking the right questions at the right time, and being able to flex your partnering style to engage C-suite executives, middle managers and front line workers effectively comes from understanding the broader industry context and the brand and business strategy.

While agreeing that the ability to craft a good sentence is hugely valuable, Laura is adamant that anyone with serious IC ambitions should first acquire a broader perspective by getting some wider business experience under their belt. She told us that one of the best ways IC professionals gain credibility is by first working in another function or part of the organization, thereby gaining a clearer understanding of different perspectives and corporate purpose and goals. Laura says it is precisely this kind of frontline experience that has made her a more effective communicator. She has formulated countless business plans and, quite simply, she knows what it's like to make – or not make – the quarterly targets and run the P&L spreadsheet, or to report back to head office when things haven't gone to plan. And that is why she has returned to IC. She has a forensic understanding of how good IC contributes to the bottom line – and a commitment to making it happen.

Imogen: How do you think internal communications is perceived today?

Laura: It depends on who's doing the perceiving! I think in the organization, strategic HR directors and informed chief executives view it as a necessity, particularly in a multicultural, multi-generational environment where they know they need to engage with different audiences, at different points, with their story, vision and direction. They also know they need help in getting the tone right and really understanding and anticipating some of the internal stakeholders' hopes and concerns. Those execs who see it as an enabling, insightful function are able to drive value through effective engagement. However, there are a few executives who misuse the skills of IC professionals, often to promote or further their own personal agendas.

In the past, I've certainly fallen into the trap of helping create a 'cult of the leader'. It's so easily done. The charismatic, visionary leader with a strong direction and probably a patriarchal, directive management style. The leader who seems to take you into his or her confidence, who offers insight and direction but in return expects little challenge and dissension. This symbiotic relationship can be very thrilling but ultimately very limiting. There is no value in being a 'yes' person. So I learnt the hard way about respectful challenge, maintaining perspective and staying true to the purpose of my role.

More broadly, the impact on the organization of a charismatic and successful leader departing, for whatever reason, can really affect shareholder and internal confidence. In this situation, it creates such a vacuum and it's very difficult for a successor to do well unless he or she adopts a clean sweep approach. IC is crucial in creating the space and setting the tone for a new leader to succeed; this can only be achieved if there is good rapport and trust between the IC leader and the new CEO. This can be difficult if the perception has been that IC has previously acted as the mouthpiece of the departed leader. So in summary, the perception of IC is really down to how well informed leaders are of its power, how strong the IC leader is in creating the opportunity to make a difference, and the level of mutual trust and respect between the leadership and the IC function.

Imogen: Where have you seen it done really well?

Laura: I think there are a lot of companies that have impactful IC functions. So often it's the magic combination of the right leadership dynamic with the IC function, clear direction or business challenge that unifies the organization and committed management. I think the challenge is sustaining impactful IC. As a function, it comes into its own in times of crisis or change, but high quality regular 'ticker tape' IC is very hard to maintain.

I think we've done well when it comes to enabling change, getting people to understand why change is happening, the proper context for it, and what it means for the company, the individual, for society in the broader sense, and what it means for customers and suppliers. For example, the IC partner in our finance function has really driven insightful, regular, functional communications, and having this as a base has allowed some of the changes we've made to be accepted more readily. Knowing that the leaders remain committed to the business strategy and goals, although the way we may achieve them can alter, provides a layer of psychological stability. Keeping the ticker tape communication of 'This is our goal and this is our progress towards that goal' is essential to maintaining focus in times of significant change. Successful IC is the ability to blend both well: the regular heartbeat communications of the company, delivered using great technology, in combination with a strong and credible change narrative.

Winds of change

Laura has extensive experience of working with a number of FTSE organizations that have embarked on substantial change over the past decade. Some of these organizations experienced significant leadership change with highly charismatic leaders and chairmen departing and significant organizational, cultural and business strategy change as a result. She has found that in this sea of change, strong organizational purpose and values provide the necessary ballast to steady employee nerves. She believes that when a business lives up to and makes its decisions based on its purpose and a set of principles, the resulting framework helps its leaders and their teams to manage work, business and life more effectively.

She shared with us one of her learning examples, working for an organization that made public its internal recruitment process between three leaders to find the successor for the CEO, who had announced his departure a year in advance. Apart from distracting internal focus away from delivering the business strategy, the organization, devoid of strong purpose, began to split into three tribal lines behind each of these candidates. After an extensive period of uncertainty and some very poor business results, the company was eventually able to attract an external CEO who came with a different, values-led approach. Laura told us that the business effectively went from being led by an innovative but seat-of-your-pants CEO to being steered by someone steeped in values-led commerce. The results, she says, were extraordinary to see. The organization shifted on its axis in the space of four weeks – a process epitomized by the CEO's invitation to engage the entire company in a conversation about what its values should be.

Imogen: How did that happen from a practical point of view?

Laura: Because of the work we'd previously done on culture and employee value proposition, and on our internal brand, I was able show him what all this research has told us, and what the organization thought of itself. Some of that he liked, some he disliked, and some he wanted to consider further. I set to work with his transition team and we came up with a hypothesis – four values and what they meant in practice. These were then shared with the executives and after incorporating their input with our people globally using our social collaboration tool we invited them to give examples of these potential values in action, and also to share any disagreement and the reasons for it. The CEO also discussed these in his travels around the organization, listening to people feedback directly on their thoughts and feelings about which of these values they saw in action and which would be a stretch to live up to. This level of openness and listening clearly demonstrated a shift in the way he expected leaders to behave: almost the first thing he did was talk about his story and why these values were important for him, and where he saw that making a difference to our potential.

Shortly afterwards the senior leaders met the top 70 leaders from across the company and they worked in small groups to use the values to develop some grey scenarios that we knew they had faced in the past – decisions that have no right or wrong answers but are decided by some moral or personal code. This was a real turning point as they could see from their conversations how their approaches differed, and how these values could provide them with a more cohesive approach to future decision making.

After this, they also received coaching on telling their own story to their people, working with us to make it credible and to become more comfortable with being open about themselves. Just after, the company undertook an extraordinary change journey that really tested the resolve of the CEO and his leaders. Luckily, we had laid the foundation with our work on values and we were much clearer about our purpose and our proposition. This put us in a strong negotiating position and enabled us to represent our people well throughout the change. During this period – which lasted well over a year – the clear behaviours of respect, fairness, honesty and openness went a long way to keeping people focused. We embarked on an approach we called 'business as planned' and the regular ticker tape communication continued alongside messages about the change.

The term 'authenticity' is often bandied around as a cliché, but the CEO and his leadership demonstrated their belief in the company – and that's what created a year of exceptional delivery. He made it clear at the beginning that he was holding his execs and broader management team to account, that he expected their commitment and support for the organization. He met and briefed them regularly throughout the change period to make sure this was maintained. Major decisions were explained at regular global town halls, backed up by company-wide e-mails and regular posts on our internal intranet, as well as the IC team preparing regular briefing papers and notes to help the execs and leadership have more in-depth conversations at local level. Many leaders also used our internal social media platform to blog, not just about what was being done but how they were feeling, giving tacit permission for people to be more open about where they were personally. This period really demonstrated our values in action. For me, keeping sight of corporate purpose and strong values has been very much about leadership at its very core – in hard and testing times.

Cracking the skills shortage

Laura's take on the millennials challenge has a very specific angle: the talent shortage in the petrochemical industry. This had been sign-posted for some time, and the forecasts pointed to it becoming an increasingly acute problem. The need to attract the brightest and best talent from university and ensure a strong skills pipeline was well established. It meant BG Group had to focus on skills development with educational institutions to encourage young people to take science, technology, engineering and maths (STEM) as degree options, and also to see the energy sector as a fulfilling career option once they'd completed their degree. The competition for those skills is not exclusive to oil and gas. Financial institutions, large consultancies, the manufacturing industry and many others are all interested in attracting the brightest and best STEM students. So how could BG Group create a differentiated employment proposition, one that made the company stand out from the competition?

This challenge was given to Laura by the Executive Director of HR, who was keen to create a unifying golden thread throughout the global talent pipeline, from attraction through to recruitment, on-boarding, engagement and, ultimately, alumni. How do you bring your employee proposition to life and create a degree of consistency in the people experience across a global organization? This was the question that defined the challenge.

There was a growing recognition that the business needed to enable mobility, to attract people who were interested in being at the forefront and cutting edge of doing innovative, challenging work, and to help them deliver this via a highly connected and knowledgeable team environment. Being able to make quick decisions and act on them was seen as a considerable advantage. This shift to the demands of a truly global organization meant a rethink was necessary. Everything, including time zone and cultural differences, now had an impact on a potential recruit's decision.

As Laura says, the old model wasn't enough. She and her colleagues knew from talking to millennials on campuses, or trying to attract them once they'd acquired two or three years' experience, that BG's proposition could be clarified and strengthened. The conversations made clear that they wanted more development prospects, more autonomy, greater opportunities to work with, learn from and influence senior experts in their field, quick decision making and better choices on interesting work on offer across the world. So, leading a small team of three, she developed a proposition underpinned with the philosophy of 'exceptional work, extraordinary people'. Laura had to fight hard to not have this become a tag line on IC people materials, believing that the BG people experience had to be felt before it was heard. To do this she identified those core people processes that would really bring the proposition to life, working with HR and external brand colleagues to shift, tweak or completely redesign these important 'touch-points'.

This work was often subtle, and required endurance as well as strong persuasion and influencing skills: colleagues were often very protective of their 'own' processes and delivery methods. Quiet perseverance began to pay off, supported by visible changes of imagery, an evolving tone and style of language, revamped internal and external social media platforms, and differing conversations in and outside the company about its culture and purpose – all with the goal of attracting the right candidates and further engaging the employees who were helping the company deliver.

One of the key discoveries about millennials has been how they respond to buddy systems – learning from each other as much as from senior leaders. We were struck by how strongly Laura felt about this, and how it has changed her own professional aspirations: a realization that much of her own development comes from what's in her 'kit bag', acquiring knowledge from the work she has done and who she is working with, rather than demonstrating what courses she has completed. Of course she'd say certificates still matter, but it's the balance between enabling people to learn on the job, observing and learning from the skills of others, and making their own contributions to other people's development, that makes the difference. That's where her 70 per cent comes from.

Laura emphasized that self-motivation and self-fulfilment are essential elements of any employment proposition for a millennial. It raises the stakes for an organization to become more transparent and to work effectively within new regulatory frameworks, which can impact considerably on how it is perceived by existing and potential employees.

Imogen: What role does employer brand play in retention?

Laura: It's essential in attracting, retaining and engaging good talent. The employer brand is implicitly linked to the employment proposition and explicitly to bringing the brand and business strategy to life in ways that are meaningful to the people who work for the company. I hope my work helps to differentiate us from our competitors in energy and other industries, and articulates what we stand for as an organization.

A good employer brand is the thread that links individual performance goals, team targets and regional or divisional strategies to the overall business strategy. It's the visual and spoken narrative that connects what an individual does to the success of the organization. And there is nothing more motivational than to know your work has meaning, that it makes a difference in some way. In this regard a strong employer brand is a key component in retention and maintaining a good internal reputation. The millennial workforce has boosted our understanding that we need to show clarity in our purpose and what we stand for in its broadest sense.

It's beyond the statements about greatest shareholder returns, fancy recruitment videos or gimmicks or snazzy give-aways; it's about having real people stand up and explicitly say, 'I am a genuine representative of the organization. This is the direction of the company, this is how I help achieve its goals. This is what it's like to work here – the good and the not so good.' Implicitly, the message is: Are you like me? Do you want to be like me? Could you work with me?

In all of our conversations we have to demonstrate our values without necessarily talking about them incessantly. You cannot massage the message in this socially connected digital era – everyone can read the Glassdoor reviews, or reach out to people who are once, twice, three times removed from the business, using LinkedIn, Twitter, Facebook and a myriad of other social media channels. We are all more networked than ever before. So companies have to pay attention, to listen and learn. And to never be complacent – to demonstrate continuous improvement even in incremental steps, encouraging employees to contribute to this as part of their job responsibility.

Imogen: How have increased regulation and the drive to greater transparency affected BG Group's business?

Laura: We must consider the regulatory, safety and environmental concerns in every country in which we operate. There is no one global regulator. To help us, we have a very strong ethical code – no bribery, corruption and so on – which we really lead on. And our business principles are built around the core of a broader ethical view on doing business with the energy industry, which affects the political, economic and social aspects of every country in which we operate.

Having a strong corporate social responsibility strategy is key. A great example is our business in Australia. Our QCLNG business constructed a 540km gas pipeline (46,200 pipes, each 1.05m in diameter – these are big pipes!) to connect the gas fields of the Western Downs to a liquefied natural gas (LNG) plant on Curtis Island. In reality this meant the business had to work with and listen to over 150 landowners to gain access for the construction of the pipeline. We did this by following a comprehensive land liaison procedure based on the principles of integrity, fairness and respect, treating every landowner as an individual and key stakeholder in the project.

Another example is in Egypt, where we were instrumental in leading the formation of a Social Performance Collaboration Forum (SPCF) with our partners to strategically manage and expand the social investment activities in Idku, a small town on the Nile that hosts an LNG facility. After helping with school reconstruction, supporting the local hospital with medical devices and helping the communities manage their solid waste, we began to better understand that local people needed a more sustainable relationship to manage a decline in their traditional livelihoods.

So the SPCF launched a stakeholder consultation exercise with the Idku community, forming the 'Ahl El Balad' project to introduce sustainable economic opportunities to local communities in the fisheries, agriculture and handcrafts sectors. We have subsequently provided training and technical assistance to farmers, fishermen and artisans, and run several capacity-building workshops with the aim of sustaining the community in the long term. We don't need regulation to make this happen.

Because of the risks associated with finding, drilling and managing oil and gas, safety is at the forefront of everything we do. Our local teams have safety moments and safety awareness briefings daily, and every meeting and briefing, in head office or anywhere in the business, starts with a safety moment – a real learning or example shared to ensure safety is at the forefront of all of our minds. Even in the office environment, away from the front line, we live by this. For example, I have experienced interventions by colleagues where I have not been paying attention while walking (I was looking at my phone) or not holding the handrail on the stairs. I have challenged colleagues and senior execs for walking up the escalators, carrying too much or talking on the phone while driving. Safety becomes a way of life and many of the practices I've learnt at work follow me into my personal life. It's ingrained in everything we do, every action, at every desk. And it's subject to such vigorous learning: we often learn lessons from near-misses or situations where unfortunate things have occurred, long before any regulator gets involved. In addition, we have more formal training in crisis management, running scenarios to help predict and prevent anything that may happen. We are not alone in our relentless focus on safety; all talent competitors in our industry are similarly focused. Safety is core to all we do.

A regular pulse

Regularity, cadence and rhythm: these are the ingredients Laura says have really replaced the tradition of the annual employment engagement survey. Regular pulse checks are essential. They provide a quick response and give individuals and managers something specific to work on. At BG, the frequency of the organization-wide survey has dropped to biannual, and now the 'Your Voice' programme focuses on capturing how likely people are to recommend working for the business, how they view the company, what can be fixed quickly and how it is performing against its values. It supplements ongoing checks to gauge what people are thinking and feeling.

Laura is an advocate of the people panel – a self-selected cross-organizational panel of employees who agree to act as the voice of the people for a set period, and who then respond to any internal survey requested by a department or function. For example, HSSE (Health, Safety, Security and Environment) might conduct a survey on safety attitudes, or IC could need to check that a piece of communication has been understood or a new channel well received. Resistant to the idea of a constant flurry of surveys landing on people's desks, Laura is convinced that this is the way ahead for allaying survey fatigue, engaging a broader network of employees and encouraging peer group conversations about topics of interest and enquiry.

Controlling that mix – the official survey and a range of supporting surveys – is essential, and requires a consistency of voice so that executives know what they are listening to. Laura is by no means alone among our interview subjects in identifying the main drawbacks of survey reliance; each one only reflects one moment in time, and that itself can be influenced by countless other factors. Timing it after the annual bonus or salary review can influence the results significantly. And we'd heartily agree that the last thing any IC practitioner would want to do is simply tell the story that executives want to hear. Beware, too, of variance. Repeating the same survey six months later could give you a completely different set of results. Pulse Checks™, she thinks, are a logical progression, and a more organized way of managing the myriad little surveys that will add up to a more realistic and accurate picture of the state of IC in your business. Then, as always, attention shifts to the outcomes.

Imogen: What about acting on the data?

Laura: Survey data must be measurable and meaningful for executives and employees. We had a tough situation back in the day – a big annual survey which entailed a lot of work. The new CEO at the time wanted us to selectively edit the results and present the data in a different way. This was a difficult position to be in, and the only way around it was to give his selective edit to the executives, and share the raw data with the level underneath, educating our local IC and HR colleagues on how to interpret it so they could partner with their local management teams on meaningful action plans and responses. The execs seemed fine with this approach – at least, no one challenged me! And it did mean that actions taken as a result of the data were useful.

This was a real learning point for me. Survey data is very powerful and it can be tempting for executives to use it as an internal political lever. Acting as the guardian of the integrity of this data is something I have fought for ever since. It's so important that a survey is autonomous and independent, and the results are reported objectively back into the organization. I do think this is easier to achieve with smaller, bite-sized surveys. It's a much more efficient way to build it in to our strategy, then act quickly and decisively. This is why short questionnaires with action-oriented outcomes and results really allow improvement. Once you've created credibility and belief that things are improving, participation rates increase, building trust and indirectly validating the data. This is another hard-won lesson: if you only rely on survey results every two years, they can take on an undue significance in the mind of investors and internal stakeholders, and influence perceptions in the wrong way.

Imogen: How do you measure the impact of IC? Can you identify a best-practice approach that is delivering demonstrable results?

Laura: I don't think you can isolate IC in this way. There are too many other factors that influence successful internal communications, including the levels of stability or change the organization faces, and its purpose and brand, culture and employee proposition. Then there's the environment in which the organization operates, plus its systems. And finally, the reputation and ability of senior leaders to lead, middle managers to engage effectively, and the levels of motivation and commitment of its workforce – how much they want to belong and contribute. IC influences and enables these aspects. It doesn't stand alone.

In with the old

It's obviously a stretch to suggest there is nothing new under the sun when it comes to effective IC. New technologies and platforms alone have proved their capacity to revolutionize comms across the board. But talking to Laura as she shared her insights, it struck us again and again how important the basics still are – for if the IC foundation is firmly in place, innovative and disruptive practices and organizational changes have a better chance of success. For Laura, straightforward measurement only tells part of the employment proposition story. It works from a performance management perspective because it helps people to understand their roles and their contribution to delivering the strategy, but it's also not systemic enough for everybody. Laura's philosophy for successful comms covers the complete picture – employee experience, employment proposition and employer brand.

Rising to the challenge, she suggested there might be too much focus on self-justification and proof of value in IC. We've all become too hung up on ROI. How about taking the value of the people as read – and moving on to a more pressing debate around how we attract, retain and engage the right talent for our business so it can deliver its brand promise and strategy? She is adamant that the most effective measures of success include: how quickly does it take a new hire to perform effectively in his or her new role? What is the average length of good performance? How much do people understand the business strategy and their role in delivering this? How credible and effective are the leaders at shaping and communicating company direction? And on brand and reputation: to what extent do people identify with the purpose and direction of the organization, including their sense of belonging and their overall levels of advocacy?

Once you've got to that point in IC, she says, you're playing a fundamental role in creating a place where people can perform effectively, where they want to work and contribute, want to do their best, and want to align with your organization's direction, purpose and values. Part of your job is attracting them, helping them understand the company and its direction so they can perform well and then letting them go when it is time for them to move on. Healthy organizations recognize that people don't want to stay forever. Ventilation, to enable internal progression and new thinking, is just as important as being able to attract the right talent. It recognizes the importance of the internal talent pipeline, encouraging development and progression and reinforcing the value of performance management systems.

For Laura, ROI focus should be on right people attraction, time to autonomy, levels of engagement and delivery rather than the effectiveness of the channel or message. For her, there are too many other factors involved in engaging and motivating people beyond a sole reliance on internal communications. And we thought that was a good prompt for us to dig a little deeper into how this part of her vision is realized at BG.

Imogen: Do you believe BG Group is effective at acting on employee feedback?

Laura: It has and hasn't been. At country level it can be extremely effective. At global level it's very difficult to achieve because what's important to someone in Trinidad is not important to someone in Kazakhstan. And what's important to someone in head office is not the same as what's important to someone in Australia.

Response to feedback is extremely effective in countries where we have strong leaders but less so where there is weaker leadership. That's what it comes down to, unfortunately. I don't think the role of corporate headquarters in responding to feedback is much more than a reporting function. Setting actions at a global level is dangerous because it's not always pertinent or appropriate for an individual operation or culture. It smacks of telling them what to do without caring whether or not it applies to them. A one-size-fits-all strategy doesn't necessarily apply in all parts of the organization. It's the same with feedback. It has to be shared and given in its local context, it has to combine that sense of what we're all trying to achieve, with an understanding of that local environment.

Where I do use broader employee feedback is in identifying those places where leaders may need more coaching in engaging their internal audiences or in other management practices. I make sure to read each individual employee comment, having these translated where necessary, as they really show a pattern of where we can best support, and also where we can use great examples in some internal narratives – using some rigorous enquiry first, of course!

Imogen: What do you like most about your role in internal comms?

Laura: No two days are ever the same, the work and the challenges are so varied. I have a fabulous team and it's great to see them develop and grow in confidence and ability as a result of all of the interesting work we get to do. I like the fact that it's strategic as well as tactical, that it's a real coaching and influencing role and that I get to work with a multitude of stakeholders across different cultures and different parts of the business. Our work drives change, reacts to change and adapts to change – as a change junkie, what's not to love about that?

Imogen: And where does it fit in your organization today?

Laura: The CEO created a new function called Safety and Sustainability – looking at all aspects of corporate reputation and the actions we take to live up to this. IC fits very nicely in here.

Based on my previous experiences, IC can sit in almost any of the corporate functions, although I would struggle with it in Legal. I've had many interesting conversations with legal colleagues about protecting the employee experience when they want us to use stiffer or more precise legal language. Of course it depends on what the organization believes is the purpose of IC. If it's fundamentally about people engagement, the employment proposition and the employer brand, then it probably does sit more strategically with HR. If it's more about promoting what the organization is doing, or looking after reputation as a whole, it probably sits well in corporate affairs. And if it's about broader brand management then it sits more neatly in the marketing function.

Imogen: What are your top three tips to anybody wanting to or working in IC today?

Laura: Do I have to stick to three?! Firstly, find an organization that is closely aligned to your personal values and aspirations. You can see this by the language and imagery they use, verbally and on their website. Look at how they organize their environment, how they treat you before, during and after interviews. This will indicate whether it's a company that you want to belong to. Always remember it's equally your choice, if you work there.

Secondly, develop a thick skin and be prepared for things to not always go quite to plan; executives are known to change their mind at the last minute, and a crisis can occur out of nowhere. You will need resilience, the ability to adapt quickly and to be able to think on your feet if you are to survive.

Thirdly, adopt a continuous improvement mindset, conduct regular lessons learnt, even with yourself (although it's almost always better with others), get regular feedback from a myriad of stakeholders about what you're doing well and could do better: take charge of your own performance. Number four is about continuous development by staying curious, listening intently, asking questions, reading as much as you can about your industry, its customers, competitors and suppliers, and by networking internally and externally. That way you'll keep building your knowledge. My fifth tip is the most important for me: IC can be a 24/7 role, if you let it, and because the work can be so engaging and seem so important, you can get lost in a sense of work first, forgetting about the balance of health and family. Don't let this happen to you. You will be far more perceptive and effective if you are well rested, healthy and an active part of wide-ranging friend and family groups. Your continued wellbeing will contribute massively to a successful, prosperous and exciting IC career.

Image consciousness

We thought we'd finish our interview with Laura by asking her about image, or more specifically, how IC could present a better face to the world, and improve the way it is perceived. After her trenchant and percipient observations, a bombshell saved to the last minute should hardly have surprised us. All the same, her declaration that she doesn't actually like the phrase 'internal communications' – finding it too narrow and limiting, and believing the function needs to be more purpose- and outcome-focused – was an incisive heads-up.

Instead, she prefers to see her fundamental purpose and role as the custodian of the employee experience. It defines her agenda and enables her to question channel choices, narratives and the intent behind messages. By focusing on people, she gets into conversations about how decisions may affect the internal stakeholders, and how they may need to think, feel and do things differently. She calls people to account for decisions, processes and messages that don't fit the employer proposition and employer brand, and that may not artic- ulate or demonstrate clearly where the organization is going. This breadth of conversations was a particularly powerful idea, which emerged several times during our interview. Equipped with her vision for the broader outcome, she feels confident about her ability to discuss with managers how they're engaging their people through change.

In short, her call to action is that we should all look beyond the old traditions of IC and consider instead how it enables the business today: from the way you communicate to bring new talent through your door, to the information and knowledge you share to make this talent quickly effective, to engaging, motivating and inspiring your talent so it develops, delivers and progresses to the best of its ability, and finally how you communicate and engage with those who leave the organization so they remain ambassadors for potential future employees. She believes that bringing to life the employer brand and employee proposition is the space where IC adds value. If you let IC only exist in its old, narrow space, you'll be searching for that elusive ROI forever.

GE Capital

05

How a coaching culture is helping
a finance company to embrace major
change and extract maximum value
from face-to-face communications
in a global structure

HELEN DEN HELD

Head of Global Communications, GE Capital

Do you really treat your team as if they are fully-fledged adults, capable of having independent thoughts and of responding in a mature and collaborative way to the responsibilities that come with the open, honest disclosure of corporate strategy and change? We don't ask this tricky question for the sake of it. We know as well as you do that the honest answer might not be as straightforward as 'Of course I do!' but our interview with Helen den Held really nailed its importance for us. In this chapter, as you will see, the issue of effective coaching as a way to generate trust and employee interaction emerged as a core element of her IC strategy. It begins and ends with the premise that your people are sentient grown-ups, eager to engage with, interpret and react to good, clear internal comms, if the mechanisms and touch-points are constantly curated and polished.

Helen is Global Communications Leader for Working Capital Solutions (WCS), which is the in-house factoring organization for GE Capital, one of the world's best known multi-sector finance companies. WCS currently employs around 1,200 people across 16 sites in Europe, Asia and the Americas. The company has been through a period of considerable change – and Helen began by telling us how this has been something of a litmus test for IC. She has previously worked in large businesses where IC was the poor cousin, and marketing and corporate comms got all the glory. As an inherently multicultural organization, WCS has valued IC as the force that pulls everyone together and engages people through the changes facing the organization since parent company GE announced that it was selling off 70 per cent of GE Capital's assets in April 2015. In the wake of the announcement, many parts of the organization were understandably unsure of their future. If IC didn't have the necessary clout, Helen told us, the process of keeping multiple teams on board through ongoing change would have been – and would still be – a much rockier proposition.

Annabel: How does your company keep sight of corporate purpose during a period of transition and how do you begin to prepare for it?

Helen: Fortunately, very quickly, GE communicated through GE Capital that certain key parts of the organization would remain – and WCS is one of those. However, it doesn't take away the angst. People still worry. At that particular moment, their basic concern is that they're no longer going to have a job.

Annabel: How did that manifest itself? How did you in your role notice that feeling, and take the temperature of the workforce?

Helen: We identified various site leaders – not managers, necessarily – who lead engagement around the 16 sites that we deal with. I had regular calls with them just to find out how things were going, what was happening on the ground, what people were saying around the water cooler. In the global organization, it's almost impossible to get that feedback.

We also set up some virtual round tables – random groups of 15–20 people in video conference with our CEO. Quite honestly, we knew that within a few months our global opinion survey was going to start, and the situation could have been disastrous for the results.

Annabel: Could you describe the exact mechanics of these virtual meetings?

Helen: They had to be video conferences so that we could actually see the people. It's all very well having people on the phone but it tends to favour the ones who speak the most. Video helps to involve people and give them all visibility. Face-to-face wins, hands down. You can read what's going on by studying expressions and body language.

Annabel: Are there any other type of moments where there's social interaction for staff at GE?

Helen: Four times a year, we arrange an all-employee meeting. We take the CEO and a number of senior leaders to one of our 16 sites and have a day onsite with the people there. There'll be round tables, discussions, a woman's network – and we'll video the all-employee meeting itself, which is really like a large town hall. From that, we create a package that is sent out to all the other global teams within a few days. They sit with a senior leader, watch the video, then ask any questions at their own local town hall meeting. It's an hour of their time, plus half an hour for their local meeting. They get to talk, they have lunch together and it creates a good vibe.

When it comes to measuring impact, I tend to call those site leaders again and ask lots of questions. How are things going? What's happening? Are we covering the right topics in our employee meetings? Are people bored stiff? What do they really want to know? Nobody's going to tell me directly. But they will talk locally, and I get that back from the site leads. Then I have people in my team who will deal one layer down, talk to the engagement people locally, who can then arrange all sorts of events and activities to discover what's on everybody's mind. We layer it.

Annabel: Do you see a variation, depending on the quality and ability of a site manager?

Helen: In a way, yes. I have realized that if someone is not happy or very engaged, that causes a bit of a dampener through the whole site. And we actually have that problem right now. It's very interesting but I'm just noticing it following the conversation that I recently had with the site leader, putting one and one together and realizing that it's not just an issue to do with the site, it's also about the leadership at that site.

Annabel: Would you look then to ask a broader range of people within that site, for their views?

Helen: Very much so, to find out what is really going on. We do various surveys after our all-employee meetings. But I find word of mouth much more powerful, because people seem to be a bit more honest. You'd think it might be the other way around, that they'd feel the anonymity of a survey might give them the opportunity to say what they want, but I don't think that's the case. You always get extremes: people absolutely love them or hate them. What I feel that I get from direct communication is that middle-of-the-road, basic honesty – and a transparency that I can then use.

Millennial differentials

Talk of transparency led naturally to the question of communicating with millennials in the workplace, which, it transpires, is a specific issue at WCS due to the organization's employee demographic. As Helen explained, much of WCS's factoring work is based on telephoning GE clients in order to be paid. Fulfilment requires large call-centre environments – and these tend to attract younger employees. In WCS's case, the average age of the workforce is late 20s (making them true millennials) and Helen feels they are driven in very different ways from their more mature counterparts, and they want more freedom than some organizations feel they can give them.

As an example, she compared two colleagues: one in her mid-30s, the other aged 24. The 10-year gap makes more difference than you might expect. The older person is comfortable with a pre-determined ballpark, and established rules and regulations. If she needs to step outside it, she'll put her hand up and say so. If Helen wants her to be more innovative or expand the ballpark, they'll have a discussion about it. The millennial, on the other hand, likes to just go ahead and do it, and doesn't see any need to put up her hand first. This is challenging to manage, but Helen also finds it inspiring because nothing really gets in the millennial's way. She has a voice and will use it. Even if that has made for an uncomfortable moment at the time, Helen has sometimes thanked her afterwards, realizing the value of the contribution. This has informed subsequent conversations – encouraging the colleague to be open with Helen herself, but also to keep in mind that there are others in the organization who don't appreciate such directness. Helen is happy with what we could dub 'The Millennial Way' – as long as it doesn't involve stepping on too many toes.

There is another important factor, which comes with the sector in which GE Capital operates: regulation and liability – bringing with them boxes that every employee has to tick, and boundaries that must be understood clearly, even when the temptation is to carry on with what suits you because it feels comfortable and you are getting the job done. There is no scope for going off-piste in that context.

Annabel: Is increased regulation and the need for transparency affecting your business?

Helen: It is and it isn't. Whilst GE Capital is no longer a SIFI (Significantly Important Financial Institution), we are still part of the PRA (Prudential Regulation Authority of the Bank of England) and we still need to operate with care and sensitivity and embrace the best practices of a regulated company. I certainly don't see us as being more regulated compared with, say, when I worked for Deloitte. There, I was the one who decided, along with a partner, if our marketing materials were on brand, and we were happy with the content. You still have to go through risk and compliance. Is that such a huge ask? I don't think so.

I think it depends on knowing your ballpark and being comfortable within in it. I suppose I create messaging that I know is acceptable within that ballpark. If there's anything that raises doubts, I'll go to Compliance or Risk and have that discussion. About 10 years ago, I worked for a couple of banks and I certainly don't feel more restricted now than I did then!

Annabel: Do you believe the annual engagement survey is dead?

Helen: To a certain degree, because it is a one-off moment in time. Last year we stopped our annual employee survey and we replaced it with a biannual survey with real-time results so employees can act on it right away. We call that 'Culture Compass'.

What I also love about GE at the moment is that we have rede-signed our performance development tool in such a way that people are requested to give each other year-round feedback. It's all about insights. We've got mobile apps, including a very cool tool that allows you to report on a discussion you might have had with your manager, for example, letting everyone know what you've been asked to focus on. It gives you structure in what you're doing, but it also keeps you honest during the year. So if your boss has asked you to do something, or if you don't like something that your manager is doing, you can use the app to communicate that back to them: 'I like this but how about doing XYZ in the future?'

Annabel: Are people being honest and open with that and using it effectively?

Helen: It is a slow process. I'm loving it. And my team is loving it as well because, as a coach, I've been coaching my people through-out the year anyway. So, we have an honest and open discussion on a monthly and weekly basis. We also have a monthly coaching discussion with one another. So, we are really very honest. They feel quite happy giving me feedback, and I feel quite happy giving them feedback.

The coaching imperative

So we arrive at the all-important c-word for Helen: coaching. Throughout our interview, we got a sustained, dynamic sense of just how central this is to her vision as an IC practitioner. Good coaching isn't just a super-grade oil for the IC machine: it is also a cumula-tive influence on the employee relationship with the organization. Every coaching touch-point has the potential to add to the reserves of experience on both sides of the relationship, storing essential insights and knowledge for the future, as well as contributing to an accu-rate contemporary picture of how well IC is performing at any given moment. As Helen put it, the only constant in any organization is change, which makes coaching people through that change a prereq-uisite for success.

She then raised the stakes in our conversation by quoting Winston Churchill: 'Courage is what it takes to stand up and speak; but courage is also what it takes to sit down and listen.' By invoking one of history's greatest leaders, she was making the resounding point that we simply don't listen well enough. Leaders, on the whole, build entire careers on developing visions and strategies around their own strongly held opinions. They aren't always such great listeners. Helen believes that coaching in any organization is about teaching managers and leaders to be better at listening – and therefore to discover what drives employees and their goals. She advocates being as passionate about what other people need to achieve as you are about your own career, and says this is central to making them feel valued and engaged. This is where the GE 'insights' approach has come into its own and has made an immediate difference. It speaks to hearts and minds on both sides of the relationship, and people feel they are being listened to – particularly when feedback is acted upon. Talk ceases to be cheap and becomes part of the lifeblood of IC.

For Helen, a great coaching culture starts with managers who epitomize the working environment they want in the organization. Sometimes that will mean listening more than speaking. They should treat their people as adults – and that means offering full disclosure on company information and change, wherever possible. They should allow reasonable mistakes without major reprimands, so that everyone learns quickly and adapts accordingly – and ends up winning.

Time is the other important aspect of good coaching: if you take enough of it to truly understand people's dreams and aspirations, you will be in a much better position to help them to achieve their goals. Warming to her theme, Helen added Albert Einstein to the mix, reminding us of one of his best-known quotes: 'If you always do what you've always done, you'll always get what you've always got.' In other words, leave your prejudgements, assumptions, biases and habits at home.

Imogen: How do you deal with some leaders who are perhaps time-poor, very focused on their end goals and the things keeping them awake at night?

Helen: Our global CEO recently told us he wanted us to identify where we don't have enough horizontal managers, and to go out and spend at least 30 per cent of our time with people. He wants us to make sure that happens because he understands that face time is worth huge amounts of money. Engagement is worth so much. If you have an organization that's really engaged, you make money and you're successful. When you have a disengaged organization, you do badly.

One of the things I loved after the 2015 GE announcement was the way the leaders communicated through GE Capital – even to people who were potentially losing their jobs. We've never had a better year than 2015! And that was because people felt they wanted to do a really good job. Yes, they probably also wanted to show themselves as being great, so that they could stay and move to another part of the organization – which many of them did.

Imogen: But do some leaders in the organization find that more touchy-feely approach is just not in their make-up? How do you get them to see the value? Surely some of them will still just not want to do it?

Helen: Of course. I had a talk with someone yesterday, a site leader. He said, 'Gosh, wouldn't it be nice if our senior leaders come to our site?' Very few of them actually get out of their room and go and talk to people. And if we knew when they were coming, we could arrange roundtable discussions, one-on-ones, seat rides (job shadowing) – where you sit next to someone and see what they actually do day-to-day. You really get to know the people and what drives them, what problems they have. And if you're not doing that as a leader you just aren't with the programme. You don't really have your people at the heart of your organization, even though they are its beating heart. If people aren't happy, your organization feels it.

Annabel: Do you believe your company is effective at acting on employee feedback?

Helen: I don't think we were, in the past. When we finished our opinion survey in September 2015, our senior leadership team all had opinions about how things could be fixed. Then we realized: it isn't about what we want and what we think the world should look like. It's about the hundreds of people in other parts of the organization. They're the ones who used the survey to complain, they're the ones who should actually form groups to tell us what we need to support.

So, we turned it; we flipped it around. We asked our Servicing Integrations Leader to form teams: Culture Compass Working Groups. She was closely involved in our internal management learning programme and she was used to hearing things 'from the horse's mouth'. She was ideal for the task and we are so lucky to have her. She decided what the pillars of the discussion were going to be and set up working groups around them. They all got together for a couple of days brainstorming, without a senior leader in sight. They left armed with all the tools to start going into the organization, interviewing people and testing their assumptions.

That group is now collaborating on various different projects to satisfy the needs of the people in WCS. And I find that is so much more valuable because we are looping back from the IC perspective, and communicating their findings and what people need to know. In our all-employee meetings, the Culture Compass team members are there to give updates and say, 'This is where we are, these are the things that are being launched.' And everybody knows that it's not just cheap talk.

Bridging the comms canyon

This combination of coaching and learning informs Helen's IC philosophy. It seemed appropriate to ask her to translate it into advice for an aspiring student of communication – somebody right at the beginning of the journey she has undertaken with such passion.

How do you know that it is the career for you? Diversify, came the answer. Helen pointed out that she came into comms from a sales and marketing background. It is only during the last 10–15 years that she has been more focused on what has become her specialism as a practitioner. The lightbulb went on when she realized there was a divide between sales and the client – a kind of comms Grand Canyon. Without knowing it specifically, communications and marketing had all the components to build a sturdy bridge: an understanding of the market, its scope and size, client knowledge, branding tools. Put them together and the divide shrinks. Then it's a straightforward stroll across the bridge by sales to say hello to the client – who now has a better idea of what you are offering – and close an easier sale.

Helen says that without her initial sales experience she might not have made the connection between day-to-day comms and the client – and this drives her every day, particularly from an IC perspective. It's about keeping clients happy, she told us, and how you keep your own people happy. Because people in your organization have to deal with those customers every single day.

Imogen: If you had carte blanche to change one thing about how WCS communicates with its staff, what would it be?

Helen: I'd love to develop an employee engagement app. It goes back to the point about the millennials. They like face-to-face far more than what you'd imagine, but they are also quite happy to get behind new technology – like Instagram, putting up photos and just feeling engaged, connected, part of a larger community, even though that community is global. I'd like that.

Annabel: What are your top three tips for anyone working in IC today?

Helen: Firstly, understand your organization because it's not all about fluffy communications. It's about what drives the business. If you don't understand how the business is making money, you will never have that seat at the CEO's table. You have to show your worth and your value.

Secondly, really understand what the issues are of people in your organization, and what drives them, so that you can communicate accordingly. Because if you're talking at too high a level, you're not going to resonate with the bulk of the people in the organization. We often make mistakes in that respect because there are so many different layers in our organization. I've had this feedback recently – that we're only communicating to the top 25 per cent. So, keep in mind that the organization is far greater than the top layer that you might be dealing with most of the time.

Thirdly, stay abreast of what's happening in the market. Have an understanding of trends: what's hot, what other companies are using from an IC perspective. We can become so bogged down by the day-to-day that we don't actually take our blinkers off and see what's out there. And go to seminars. Hear what speakers are saying. Those little nuggets of information go a long way.

Annabel: What kinds of things inspire you at the moment? What do you read or listen or tune in to?

Helen: I read a lot around coaching. I'm realizing more and more how change affects people. And because it has such a major effect on people, it has an effect on your organization and the temperature in your organization. There are three books in particular that I'd recommend: *Coaching Essentials: Practical, proven techniques for world-class executive coaching,* by Patricia Bossons, Jeremy Kourdi and Denis Sartain. This book offers practical coaching techniques for almost any situation and is well-indexed for ease of use; *Coaching for Performance: GROWing human potential and purpose – the principles and practice of coaching and leadership,* by John Whitmore; and *Time to Think: Listening to ignite the human mind,* by Nancy Kline – a book that teaches people how to listen, giving others the time to think and get the best out of every situation.

Annabel: Let's talk about remote working. How do you communicate with your workforce when they're off site?

Helen: What we've realized at GE is you really can work from anywhere. A big part of our WCS population do have desks because it's call-centre type work, and they'll be in the office. But other parts of the organization could be anywhere and they will have laptops with embedded cameras. We have Cisco WebEX for sharing documents and video conferencing. My own team is remote. They're in the United States, I'm in the United Kingdom. I don't care where they happen to be – but that's me. There are other people in our organization who prefer to have people in the office. But you'll probably find that they are people who have grown up in an organization that was very face-to-face, without global teams. For me it doesn't matter where you are.

Remote working has its merits but also has its downside – you might not feel at one with the organization at times. You'll miss things if you're not part of the water cooler culture. And it doesn't matter how small your team is – you miss an awful lot if you're not in the office regularly.

Compelling stories

Missing out on news, events, messages – in short, missing out on the ongoing narrative of the organization – is certainly a potential debit in the IC account, but as Helen told us, often this is less down to being physically present in the workplace and more about the way a company tells its story internally and engages all of its people in the constant development of the plot. Keeping it fresh and alive so that everybody wants to play their part is crucial and, quite bluntly, Helen admitted that WCS has been 'pretty bad' at story-telling until now. Building a narrative that everyone can speak to in the same way is now a core element of her IC strategy.

The challenge is to pull together a complete and engaging story from the individual strands of the organization that are often engaged in such different operations. We could quite understand how difficult this makes it to achieve a single narrative. From such complexity Helen has identified the fact that it's ok to own your own little bits of the story – and these can be different. One size doesn't have to fit all. This is a tricky challenge for anybody who is trying to make IC the unifying force within an organization, particularly at a time of transition. It is a work in progress for Helen, for the time being.

Imogen: Where do you see WCS in five years' time? Do you think it will be communicating differently with its staff or will it be just an evolution of what you're already doing now?

Helen: I think it might be an evolution of what we're doing now. I hope we are a lot more transparent and that will definitely happen with our new performance development tool. And I'm hoping that we'll be far more reactive to people's advice and proactive about putting it into action.

Imogen: How about personal situations and how they impact the way you communicate at work?

Helen: I remember a conversation I had with my father when I was probably in my teens. I asked him, 'Why do you stay with that big organization? Because, you obviously don't like working there. You never have anything nice to say about them. Why don't you go off to Saudi Arabia instead?' And he replied, 'Because I've chosen to be with my family.' And I said, 'Well, sorry, dad. Very big of you. But, you know, quite honestly if I'm really unhappy with an organization, I'll just leave.' And he said, 'Well, we'll talk about that when you're older.'

I'll be honest, when I have been really disillusioned with an organization, I have left. And I may have made a couple of rash decisions in my career just because I felt I needed to change. I would advise anyone in their career to really sit down and to ask themselves a whole bunch of different questions: is it just an itch you need to scratch now, is it really an issue, or is it something that can wait? I'm a little older, a little wiser now.

Imogen: From an internal communications perspective, it is interesting in terms of how you bring the personal into work. You're there to work. And yet it's the personal that creates the bond and builds the trust, isn't it?

Helen: I absolutely agree with you. Many years ago, when my mother died, I came back to work after her funeral. A colleague came in and started talking to me, telling me that she'd also lost her mother some time before, and that she really understood what it was like. I started crying, and apologized for that. And she said sorry but she was going to say something really bluntly; she was Dutch so we were used to that! But she said, 'I'm so glad that you're showing a human side of you, because you never do!'

I've just had a coaching discussion with a communications manager. We were talking about personal branding and I asked her, 'Who are you really?' She said, 'Well, I don't really bring my whole me to the office.' I replied, 'Well, why not?' I've noticed since I had that reality check 12 years ago, that the more you show your vulnerability, the more people engage. Now, there is no office me and home me. It's just me. These days, I'm the crazy one who sometimes comes into a meeting, looks at what a colleague is wearing and says, 'Great shoes' – then carries on talking about the matter in hand. I don't give a hoot because it's those things that make you the person that you are: a little bit off the wall, a little bit crazy, a little bit vulnerable, inspiring. Whatever you'd like to call it – charisma, perhaps – it shows itself in different ways with different leaders.

I think if more leaders came to the office and were more themselves, you would find that you'd create a far more authentic organization; and you'd achieve so much more because you'd cut through the nonsense, just by being yourself. A lot of it is about baggage, or people just trying to hide themselves – a lack of confidence or whatever. And they're hiding behind this huge wall, which they feel they have to put up around them before going into the office every day. You can have some really ground-breaking conversations when people do start changing and they are honest, open and vulnerable.

Propaganda: there's a word I've been using so often recently. Let's cut through the propaganda machine which is internal communications, telling us that everything is just rosy – because everything isn't rosy. And all your staff members know that. So, whenever we have meetings, we talk about things that have gone wrong and how we've managed them, and how we've learnt from those mistakes – or maybe learnt quickly and moved forward.

That's one of our GE Beliefs: Learn and adapt to win. Because it's not just about learning. You have to adapt and carry on, and make it work. We all make mistakes, we're human. At the same time, the days are gone when you can just say, 'Let's hide behind it. Let's just pretend it never happened and let's move on.' No. Be vulnerable and acknowledge the mistake – because otherwise all you are being is that propaganda machine!

Make it personal

Helen combined some intensely personal recollections and tough business sensibility with a freedom unique among the top practitioners who have given so freely of their wisdom for this book. It was genuinely moving and inspirational to hear her weaving these two, traditionally separate, aspects of a senior executive's life together with such grace and skill – and we can see how that capacity must translate into the culture of openness and supportive culture she is helping to develop in GE Capital's brave new world. She hit the mark when she pointed out the difference between the statement, 'I want to give you feedback,' and the question, 'Can I give you feedback?' – the difference between a brusque command and an invitation to consider doing something differently.

For Helen, there is never any need to hide behind words. There will usually be a nicer way to say things – even if you are delivering bad news or having difficult conversations. Consider your words carefully and you can hold an impactful conversation, walk away feeling better, and not leave the other person feeling that they've been attacked. Mutual respect can go a long way to cutting through the analytical challenges faced by many organizations today.

This sensitive approach to IC has been honed and reinforced by Helen's experience. As she told us in conclusion, as part of the senior leadership team she knows all the issues – strategic and business – that have to be addressed. She's in the fireplace of the business – it gets hot sometimes, and you hear things you don't necessarily want to. But hear them you will. What matters is how you respond to them, and how your response manifests itself with the people who must manage the consequences. Treating them like adults is a great way to start.

References

Bossons, P, Kourdi, J and Sartain, D (2009) *Coaching Essentials: Practical, proven techniques for world-class executive coaching*, Bloomsbury, London

Kline, N (2002) *Time to Think: Listening to ignite the human mind*, Cassell, London

Whitmore, J (2013) *Coaching for Performance: GROWing human potential and purpose – the principles and practice of coaching and leadership*, 4th edn, Nicholas Brealey Publishing, London and Boston

Heathrow Airport

06

How one organization is effecting major cultural change and developing a new generation of leaders by empowering its people to understand their own strengths – and align themselves with company values

VICKIE SHERIFF

Director of Communications, Heathrow

Cinderella might finally get a formal invitation to the ball if Vickie Sheriff's vision for the future of IC becomes reality. As Director of Communications at Heathrow Airport, she speaks from the height of a distinguished career in comms. Even before our interview, she nailed that vision in our Pulse Check™. When we asked how IC is perceived as a profession today, her response was precise and succinct: senior executives, she said, now realize that an engaged workforce is a productive workforce. The momentum being generated by that realization – and its impact on the evolution of IC as a profession in its own right – turned out to be a major theme in our conversation.

Vickie previously looked after global communications at drinks multinational Diageo, and before that was Director of Group Communications at the Department for Transport. With this depth of experience, she clearly has IC running through her veins today. She identified a definite shift in its perception and value within the business, and we wanted to hear her insights into how this plays out in a dynamic, fast-moving environment such as Heathrow, where her current responsibility for media relations, PR and strategy affords her a unique overview. We certainly weren't disappointed. An engaged workforce, she told us, is made up of individuals who are truly aligned to what a company's doing and feel they have a voice. They feel they know what's going on and the communications are sincere.

Annabel: How well do you think IC is perceived as a profession, generally and at Heathrow?

Vickie: For a long time it has been the Cinderella of communications – and often the victim of huge demands from within the business, particularly from senior folks who come from a 'broadcast' perspective. They think 'Get the message out' is the most important thing. However, it is changing as a function. We're getting some very good communicators in the IC space. I've been fortunate to work with some top notch internal comms professionals. Change is happening because IC is attracting these higher calibre people. The conversations are weightier, and the workforce is more engaged, aligned and productive.

In order for people to feel engaged, they need to feel they're being valued as individuals, and communicated with in a way that is relevant to them, in a tone of voice that's attractive to them. They need to feel they are part of the conversation, not simply on the receiving end of messages that have been broadcast from higher up.

IC does have a role in terms of providing information and that's why it is often well connected with HR. But it also has a big role in aligning people to the organization's vision and what it is trying to achieve. Great conversation is the sweet spot for IC.

Annabel: How do you deliver the best IC within an organization through a period of transition? How have you helped the company to keep sight of corporate purpose and employees on track?

Vickie: I don't think I know an organization that isn't engaged in some form of change.

You can't have really clear purpose unless the chief executive is able to articulate the vision that supersedes it clearly and concisely. I think at Heathrow right now, people know the vision well, and it underpins our business plan: 'To give passengers the best airport service in the world.' And they are particularly aligned to the corporate purpose that activates the vision. It's part of the culture, a mantra if you like, and is very simple: 'Making every journey better.'

They're also trying to change the organization so that it's led by people who are attached to Heathrow's values and purpose as well as their own. People have to walk through what Heathrow's purpose is and what it means to them. This is a big cultural change that's taking place now. There's a real sense that if people can align themselves with the company – its purpose and its values – and they really understand what their own purpose and values are – what makes *them* tick – they will become more engaged, more productive, and they can be better and more genuine leaders as well as getting us on the road to achieving the company's vision.

Annabel: Do you run the cultural immersion and personal insights training internally or do you use external change consultants who come in and work with new recruits?

Vickie: Our training programme was created with the help of an external facilitator but is run by the people who work in the organization. They've now rolled out another programme that is developing our people by providing them with coaching skills, starting from the senior leadership all the way down through the organization. Again it is being run by the people who work in the organization. It builds on the individual's knowledge and understanding of their own and the company's purpose and values with a view to developing successful leaders.

Millennial disruption

In her pre-interview Pulse Check™, Vickie's forthright and passionate assessment of the impact of millennials in the workplace really caught our attention. They are more motivated by values, she explained. They want to be part of delivering the message and part of the conversation rather than just being communicated at. Because they are more driven by experience and demand more from their own roles, the impact manifests itself across the board – from the way technology is used in IC to the type of contracts that define their job expectations, and the need for Heathrow to satisfy their career progression.

It was a theme that she quickly warmed to in the interview, having recently emerged as one of the dominant topics at a corporate planning session involving the whole comms team. When they were asked what they think will change over the next five years, the rise of the millennials as a significant part of the workforce was identified as one of the major challenges, especially in terms of their behaviour. They are self-centred, Vickie said, and that is not a bad thing. They are just more focused on themselves. They are values-driven and less likely to be as corporate-oriented as their longer-serving colleagues. The corporate life is not what they aspire to. Instead, they want genuine conversation and communication, to be ambassadors and part of the channel. They don't want to be broadcasted at. This might sound like a precocious list of demands but Vickie's excitement about the benefits these new attitudes and expectations bring to IC was palpable. It was fascinating to hear how they are rippling out across the organization, in an environment where technology and Big Data are increasingly taken for granted.

Annabel: How do you manage the impact of millennials in the workplace?

Vickie: They expect more from work. They are perhaps less loyal than previous generations. They want something out of it, and that's why values are really important to them. I believe this is in part due to the fact that they're of a generation that had to invest massively in their education to get where they are. Before, people would have gone to university with a grant and no fees to pay. They have made significant personal investments in improving their own worth and basically, unconsciously, they want to see a return: to be trusted, involved, to have responsibility, without any corporate whitewash.

There are a few other big differences to note, for example in the way they communicate and use technology. The rise of social media is a really big part of this. For millennial communication, think mobile first! We're catching up. How do we meet their needs, communicate with people and get where we want to get to? All this is going to affect the structure of our organization as we look at the next five years.

It's not just millennials. The way the communication is changing now means the written word is never good enough for a very visual culture. We always seek to work in a visual way, not just in words. We see people are time-poor and they want to be attracted and entertained very quickly. Their attention time is really short. They can't be bothered to read long-form, written work anymore. They want to see things visually. They want to be able to absorb information very quickly. Information has to be of interest, engaging, entertaining and answer 'So what?' The challenge for us is, often, how on earth do you think about taking a bit more of a risk to be engaging, and make comms stand out against a backdrop of risk-averse corporates?

Annabel: You mentioned technology and mobile first. Are there any other types of technology or apps that you're using?

Vickie: We've had mobile at Heathrow for some time. One of the interesting challenges for communications, and I don't think it's just Heathrow, is how your IT department reacts and responds to the technology that we're given. For example, we've created an app, but when staff mobile phones were changed, their apps no longer worked. Sometimes, demands from comms and technological capabilities are not aligned, and IT has to play catch up. We're getting over that.

What's also becoming very clear is that people don't want two devices – their own and the one provided by the company. We're moving to a situation where we need to produce apps and platforms that can be used on people's own devices, and cheap wearable technology that they can still access at times that suit them.

Annabel: What is the most successful app that you're using that people have bought into?

Vickie: We have an app that is currently being redeveloped. It provides employees with news and information. Also, we're just moving to Microsoft's Windows 365 platform, which gives a lot more ability for two-way communication, using things like Skype and other tools that come with it. Our people are not sitting in front of a computer. We're a very operational organization and we have thousands of front-line employees like security officers, customer liaison staff, people who manage trolleys.

Annabel: How are regulation and the need for transparency affecting the role of IC at Heathrow?

Vickie: Transparency and Big Data are big cultural shifts that every organization is going through – and it's the right thing. There is a demand on companies to be honest and to share things. It raises questions around what people need to know, what they want to know, and whether or not something should be available for them to access or be aware of – because of commercial confidentiality, for example.

Big Data is naturally a 'big thing' because, like many companies, we have collected lots of data through internal research and through contacts with customers. We can be a lot smarter with understanding and using it. The downside of Big Data is regulation and the major risks and responsibilities it carries. It creates the opportunity for customization and the ability to do some things – people want the personal touch. But they also want to be reassured that that data is not being misused at all. How you work with that data is really very important and carries with it responsibility.

Exaggerated rumours

Rumours of the death of the annual employee engagement survey form one of the central motifs of the interviews we carried out for this book. Is it or isn't it breathing its last? We will save reaching a consensus for later, but as far as Vickie is concerned, those rumours seem to have been exaggerated. Indeed, at Heathrow, the annual staff survey is alive and kicking, but as IC evolution gathers pace, it is equally clear that its role is also shifting and increasingly augmented by regular mini-pulses that provide the immediacy that once-a-year engagement simply cannot deliver. It is, as Vickie told us, literally just a snapshot – as she put it elegantly, a barometer that captures the temperature of one moment in time. While it produces rich data for year-on-year comparison, allowing for the measurement of progress and exposing day-to-day issues, it is also essential for the organization to check the temperature – and capture the underlying stories – between times.

Vickie told us that despite the undoubted cynicism around the annual survey – a lingering, anecdotal sense that in completing it, people are going through the motions rather than making their voices heard – there is real value in it for the business. Some units give very honest feedback. It points to good trends and flags issues that demand closer attention. Most important of all, says Vickie, is that it is treated with genuine interest rather than just a competition – to beat last year's figures, or the other business units' scores – so that the scores are meaningful.

It is essential that the processes to address specific issues are equally genuine. Quite bluntly, Vickie asked us, how many times has the question arisen in our experience of senior leaders saying one thing and not following through? We didn't have to go too far back in our collective memories for the answer. A genuine, engaged process works from the top down and from the bottom up, said Vickie, allowing issues to be identified and addressed. That's where the annual survey is most valuable, although it isn't necessarily easy, and it remains a core tool in the professionalization of IC for the insight it provides.

> **Annabel:** What advice would you give to an up-and-coming comms professional about how to make a genuine pathway between what's going on and actually taking action?
>
> **Vickie:** It's a year-round thing. Make sure that people understand what comes out of it (the annual survey). If they've invested time and effort to do it in the first place, they need reassurance that there's value in doing it again and that's the organization's responsibility. It doesn't replace face-to-face time with managers. There needs to be evidence of 'You said, we did it.' So there's that side of it too and this has to be a year-round plan, aligned to the company's vision, purpose and values, that's genuinely co-owned by the people it involves.

Annabel: Can you expand on what you mean when it comes to face-to-face line management?

Vickie: Nothing will replace good old face-to-face communication. When there's a failure or a message block, either coming up from people in lower management roles or between the front line and their seniors, it's often because there's no face-to-face engagement. Instead, there's an over-reliance on organized or 'broadcast-only' IC channels.

I have seen this in many organizations: middle-level management can unintentionally be the block for good internal comms. Perhaps it happens because junior staff are promoted into middle management in very hierarchical organizations. They're not *quite* senior managers and they haven't *quite* left the ranks of their pre-management days when they were the 'done-to's' – ie waiting to be told what's going on and what to do, without being quite trusted enough to know why. So when such folks reach management roles, they have a built-in cynicism and no buy-in into 'senior management messages'. It's perpetuated by organizations not being open and honest with their comms, and not having suitable channels and opportunities for genuine conversation. People can generally deal with difficult messages or things they can't change, as long as they have an opportunity to be heard. It's about the organization being very clear about the important role of managers as communicators and helping them in this regard.

The staff survey can help identify if there is that 'block'. Organizations that don't invest much in training people will tend to focus their training budget on the talented leaders and future leaders and not the rump of middle management. An understanding of, and investment in, middle management is a critical aspect of keeping IC channels open and strong.

I've already talked about purpose and values here at Heathrow and we are now in a second wave of giving people throughout the organization the skills to coach and lead. I believe that if you help people get the skills themselves it is really empowering and motivating and helps your internal communications. Investing in people is Heathrow's way of trying to address the question of 'How do we get the best out of our staff?' In the past it was often a case of telling them what to do, the old 'command and control' model.

Wider horizons

Vision is one thing but sooner or later in IC you run into the need to measure impact and outcomes. Without that measurement, it is impossible to move on to a new phase of enlightenment. The cycle may be repeated but it should always be in the light of exciting new discoveries and revelations. Vickie gave us a dynamic picture of how this process pans out at Heathrow – a work that is constantly in progress. It soon became obvious that this degree of enthusiasm for the day-to-day detail of IC could give all of us an inspirational blueprint for development.

She described a steady round of ad hoc reviews and staff focus groups that help to identify what's working and what isn't. Metrics are used to measure who's looking at which internal messages, which ones are working better online, how long people are spending on them, which are popular and which are languishing unloved. From this, a clear idea of what people want emerges and is constantly refreshed: vital at Heathrow where the plan is to move from providing IC to 6,500 people, to delivering it to the entire 76,000-strong airport community. They might be employed by different organizations but the vision is to create a team sense across the entire workforce – team Heathrow – whether they are working for a cleaning company, the in-flight caterer or an airline. In other words, major changes are afoot and we were eager to hear how this vision will open IC up to a wider audience. Clearly, it's going to be a big job.

> **Annabel:** This must signal a big change in terms of output. How do you make the people who aren't directly employed by Heathrow but work at the airport feel part of an engaged family? What will be the first stages in that step-up to a larger audience?

> **Vickie:** This will be technology-driven. We are in the throes of getting the right platform so that we can have an app targeted to specific groups. People like to have apps for news or comms tailored to their interests. Audiences are really segmented. That's the trend. And specific apps are part of the way forward.

> The second thing is content, which signals a different structure for us. Now, internal and external comms are really just one and

the same because you are story-telling – people to people. Often, what's interesting internally is interesting externally – and a story for the internal audience is probably suitable for an external audience too.

At the airport we look at audiences: everyone from our own people and our passengers, to members of the local community and politicians. We look at what each audience does, how our message will land with them, and how they like to interact with us. What's the right content for us to produce and deliver via the channels that they will want to look at and engage with? The old days of static lengthy newsletters on the website and press releases are gone. We have to work in a different way. It's now about delivering engaging content with a consistent message, in the right tone, in the way that people want to be communicated with, that allows them to have a conversation. That means we have to be much better at planning in order to land the right messages with the right audiences, because producing engaging content – video, graphics, images, micro-sites – is also costly.

This is really about how we change our organization. You have to be robust and sometimes say 'no' to the internal demands that always come up, as well as developing the skills agenda – it can only work if you have the right people with the right skills.

Most of our IC content is generated by our internal communications team. That's really darned good. They are pretty much self-taught, producing scripts, making and editing video. We're looking at podcasts too. We do use external suppliers as well, but we're producing a lot of engaging content ourselves. We'd like to move to a model whereby it's a central resource for external comms too. From the start, it's really all about which audience we're talking to and what will they find engaging, while getting our message across.

Annabel: What is your top tip for an aspiring IC professional?

Vickie: Just remember that people want to communicate in a way that engages them. They want to be a part of the conversation. So think about how you're going to have that conversation. I think that's a challenge for us all.

Annabel: What do you least like about your role in IC?

Vickie: Micromanaging! I see the volume of work that is going through internal comms. It's just staggering – great work that should be valued more by the organization and not overused. Too often IC is seen as an overhead to be scrimped on. There's an attitude that everyone can take a photo and write, can't they? Things have started to change but there's still a long way to go.

Annabel: Where do you get your inspiration from?

Vickie: I'm somebody who just loves learning from other people. You never stop. For example, it's been a couple of years since I last went to an IC-specific conference but I'm still benefiting from what I learnt there. To me it doesn't matter what form that learning takes – I just love hearing about the things that others have achieved and tried – it's of huge value. You can either be inspired or nick their ideas!

Hearts and minds

In our pre-interview Pulse Check™, when we asked Vickie how good Heathrow actually is at acting on employee feedback, she was candid in acknowledging a familiar IC conflict: the visionary and progressive 'You say, we do' approach versus the fact that it often has to be delivered by and to people who find change difficult and have low expectations of success. We wanted to take the opportunity to press her further on this, and her response was a concise critique of broader corporate culture: no company is really brilliant at processing staff feedback, but demonstrating that you are trying is genuinely important. This is the IC equivalent of putting your money where your mouth is, and it cuts to the heart of Vickie's passion for changing – indeed, disrupting – the status quo by using the information generated by a new comms strategy. This sounded to us like a compelling, self-fulfilling prophecy.

Successful IC, she told us, is all about stories and people, and that fundamental realization is changing the way Heathrow communicates with its staff. As an organization and an environment, it can seem efficient and cold – all about runways and flashy terminals, the aspects that have tended to dominate discussion of one of the world's busiest airports. People end up being the missing link in the story-telling, and it's exciting to be able to put them back at the heart of the comms strategy. They trust other people who look and sound like them.

That could be a reason why research tells us that a CEO's voice is less trusted than other people's, particularly if he or she talks in very corporate language. If that CEO is overused in the organization's IC, it could be at the expense of people who would tell a more vivid and engaging story. In other words, you need to win employees' hearts as well as their minds. It's just a matter of finding people in the business who can engage through comms rather than spouting messages. They're the ones who will give voice to the practitioner's vision and extend it so that it's about more than just words within the business: it's also about bridging internal messages with the outside world, just making sure that somebody's individual achievements are celebrated in the local paper, for example.

Vickie offered the British Army as a model example of an organization where everybody is trained to the ultimate level to fulfil their role, from the top general to the soldiers on the ground. They become the experts and are therefore the best story-tellers and media spokespeople. Soldiers won't be interviewed about defence spending or operational decisions, but they can talk genuinely and authentically about their own activities to the people who will find it meaningful and trust them, be they the public or their colleagues. This, she says, is a valuable lesson to take into corporate life. We couldn't agree more. Along with the need for a demonstrable passion for what is starting to look like a revolution in IC, and the imperative of embracing the disruptions introduced by the millennial workforce, we'd suggest it is among the most resonant take-aways from Vickie's rich compendium of insights.

Just

07

How a brave and bold approach to internal communications is supporting a merger at the innovative retirement income specialist – and building channels that exploit the millennial world of social media to the max

JENNY BURNS

Director of Brand and Customer Experience, Just

Give Jenny Burns a crisis and she's in her element. She offered this revelation mid-way through our interview, almost apologetically, before warming to the theme. Crisis, she told us, is when internal comms thoroughly comes into its own. As an IC leader, you have to be the person who keeps everyone calm, who knows what to do – and who does it quickly, all the while ensuring that other leaders remain calm and do the right things. On reflection, we don't think there is anything 'awful' – her word – about Jenny's admission. Quite the contrary. With 22 years' IC experience under her belt, she was simply zooming in on a vital aspect of the function: how to harness the adrenalin that kicks in when a specific challenge arises.

Jenny's confession that she loves a crisis emerges from that depth of experience, which sadly includes the sobering memory of being in Canary Wharf when the 7/7 London bombings took place in 2005. She recalled being in the lift, descending to the Corporate Affairs department on the 10th floor, fielding an anxious call from her husband about what appeared to be a major electrical failure in the city, and arriving back at her desk to find the computers down and news about the attacks spreading. 'There was that moment of personal fear, impacting on me,' she told us. 'But then you switch. Your primary focus is to keep your team calm and assess what needs to be done. Get them focused on the task in hand. We had our retail bank CEO on the tannoy reassuring everyone that they were safe where they were, and that boats and buses would be arranged to get them home. Above all, the message was "Don't worry". It was a long day. Really long. I got home exhausted. But to feel that you've played a part in that and helped to keep people safe – well, I think we did the right thing from an IC perspective.'

Journey of a lifetime

Those 22 years represent a fascinating journey and as Jenny talked us through it, we could see how she values the very different insights and experiences accumulated at each stage. She started her career at retailer WH Smith, where she moved into comms as part of the firm's management programme. She has never looked back, building a passion for IC in particular because she believes it has an impact on business performance at every level.

After 10 years she joined Barclays Bank, moving from a company where she had first-hand experience of every process to being part of a global organization with 125,000 employees. This is where she feels she cut her teeth from an IC perspective, earning rapid promotion and working with Roger Davis, who ran the retail bank at the time, to support his comms strategy: essentially, she was a smaller cog in a much bigger wheel. It was a steep learning curve, plunging her into working life in London and in at the deep end of the financial services sector.

From there, Jenny went to British Gas, where she worked incredibly closely with managing director Phil Bentley during a very tough time for the business, which was undergoing a huge transformation programme. The employee engagement challenge was immense, she told us. 'People were embarrassed to say they worked for British Gas because there was so much bad press at that time,' she remembered.

'Phil and I just gelled really well together and spent a couple of years successfully turning that business around. Today, it's again being accused of not being customer-focused because of the amount of money it's making – which is a bit sad to see.'

After British Gas, Jenny joined HBOS for six months in 2008, timing her arrival perfectly to coincide with the global financial crisis that took the UK banking system almost to the point of meltdown. After a brief but highly educational stint there, she left to head up group IC at Telefónica O2, a fascinating shift, because she was now working for a major brand-led organization that emphatically put its customers first. It was an exciting time for the business, which included the signing of an exclusive iPhone deal and the branding of the O2 arena (previously known as the Millennium Dome), and a challenging time for employee engagement, particularly with an army of customer service advisers to keep on board and supporting such rapid commercial growth. Like a magpie on a constant quest for new comms jewels with which to stud her skill set, Jenny then spent five years at RSA Insurance, where she built expertise in another sector new to her, rose from UK to group responsibility, and extended her range into brand communications and social media.

Jenny has spent the last 12 months rising to the challenge of a major business rebranding exercise. Two fierce competitors, Just Retirement and Partnership Assurance, came together to form Just. Jenny developed a new brand visual identity and proposition from scratch to create a beacon for customers in the confusing world of retirement.

After covering such a comprehensive CV, we were hardly surprised to hear that Jenny is now fully embracing the challenge of a major business rebranding exercise, not to mention the multiple IC demands that come with it. In short, this couldn't be a better time to get a Burns-eye view of the state of the IC landscape.

Annabel: How is internal comms perceived as a profession today?

Jenny: That's a great question. It's changed. If you go back 22 years, I don't think it was seen as a profession at all, and prior to that, it was probably seen as an aspect of desk activity from an HR perspective. But I think that particularly during the last 15 years, anyone engaged in internal communications has played a tremendous role in actually convincing businesses that it is absolutely fundamental to their operation – and demonstrating how it feeds into the performance of the business.

Today, IC is seen as a profession in its own right. It isn't the poor relation to PR and marketing any more, and I think that more and more, CEOs – particularly at the FTSE 100 and 250 level – see it as an absolutely critical asset for their directors and teams. You know, as cost pressures grow you need to do more with less, and it's there we need higher engagement and higher productivity. I think IC has become central to that.

Annabel: How would say your company keeps sight of corporate purpose during a period of transition or merger?

Jenny: It depends which one you're going through: they're two different things but the methodology can be the same. During any kind of change, companies can have a tendency to shy away from continually communicating the corporate purpose for a few reasons: fear that corporate purpose will change because of that merger; fear that in the same communication, you're talking about something positive and about saving costs, which almost always has an employee implication. I'd argue that you need to make sure those people you want to retain are engaged, while being respectful of the cost message and the fact that other people are potentially being made redundant. It's vital to keep that consistent corporate message going. And actually it's the beacon and rationale for the change. It has to be the drumbeat.

Annabel: We're having this conversation six months into your new role at Just Retirement, with the merger going through. How is this playing out tactically on the ground?

Jenny: It's tough, because the entire business is in consultation, so there is effectively a risk of redundancy. But what we are doing is talking about the positive aspects of the integration and balancing that with the things that are going to impact on people.

What generally happens in this kind of situation is that there is a big proportion of money that you need to save as a result of the merger – and it certainly applies in our case – but you also get investment in order to make that saving. So it's about helping people to understand that they're going to be part of an organization that is still going places, and still growing. This gives us the opportunity to invest in things like systems that might have lacked investment in the past – and that's a really positive message for those people who are going to stay with the business.

We've called the integration programme 'Fusion'. We've given it a brand, we've given it a name, and we've developed associated channels around it that give people some hope and are exciting: channels that they can get involved in, such as Fusion TV. This will be presented by an employee who volunteers for the role; they'll be celebrating the successes and key milestones of the project, as well as providing support for people who are going to be experiencing the changes. We're also helping people update their LinkedIn profiles. That's good for us as a business, from a brand perspective, but it also helps employees who maybe, sadly, will have to seek other opportunities. There are definitely some tactical things you can do to help to foster and retain an understanding and appreciation of corporate purpose.

The honorary millennial

At this point in our conversation, Jenny let slip another revelation: she considers herself an honorary millennial. She has long held this emerging generation of talent in high regard for the freedom and flexibility they generate through their use of social media platforms, and clearly identifies with their capacity for innovation – virtually on the fly. Capturing and exploiting this capacity to streamline IC channels has become a key driver in her own approach to meeting today's challenges, which has its roots in her insurance years at RSA. There, she told us, IC enjoyed a great success with the corporate social media platform Yammer: about 10,000 messages were posted every month. Jenny credits millennial employees in the customer service environment with kick-starting that mini revolution, and says it effectively gave them a voice to instigate change around the delivery of customer service. The claims environment, she pointed out, is where the moment of truth occurs in the customer experience for any insurance company. Employees on the front line in the call centre bore the brunt when the company got something wrong, resulting in frustrated staff and dissatisfied customers. Yammer gave them a comms channel to make process and policy changes internally, leading to an improved customer experience. Used in this way, it becomes a really powerful tool, giving employees a direct channel back into the business.

Millennials, Jenny said, expect information in completely different ways from other people in the organization. They expect more transparency and openness, and they expect to be communicated with at speed – something that Jenny feels IC practitioners have been in denial about for a long time. There's little point in taking the time to draft a communication and send it when it's ready or the time is deemed right, if the grapevine has already been busy delivering the message via other, quicker channels. If you can't keep up, you'll soon start to disengage people. Yammer is simply a great internal social channel that is basically free and easy to use. Millennials get it – and are probably best placed to help older generations, who are less used to its speed, to engage with it. They can, said Jenny, be IC-enablers from the bottom up, playing a successful role in influencing the evolution of new comms channels in the business.

Annabel: How are increased regulation and the need for transparency affecting your business?

Jenny: Hugely. It's been fascinating because I have always worked in the regulated environment – and Just Retirement only went through its IPO two years ago. So there's still a lot of talk within the business about the good old days when we weren't regulated and didn't have to answer to shareholders or report to the City, which meant we could be totally transparent internally.

I've found the impact of regulation more profound here than I expected. People talk about it a lot. I've long since got used to a regulated environment but I've noticed how it really impacts on us now: you can't be as transparent as you'd like to be with your employees, and that gives the impression that you're not trusting people with information. It creates the perception of a slight distrust between management and employee. I think internal communicators have to work harder to bridge that gap. So something I'm doing here is to establish what KPIs and measures we can talk about, outside the regulated environment, that will give people a sense of progress without going against the rules.

Then, from a brand and IC perspective, we want people to particularly understand and engage with our demographics: our customer base is 55-plus. We want our people to use their judgement when they're talking to a client because, if you're in your 80s and you've got a policy with us, you may need more time on the phone. We might have to depart from the script in order to provide you with genuinely individual help. Our people need to understand the project they've embarked on with us, and what that means for them.

Regulation does hamstring us slightly in terms of wanting to do the right thing for the customer. But I think we're really good at making sure people understand what the minimum requirement is, and that beyond that they can use their judgement.

Annabel: Do you believe the annual employee engagement survey is dead?

Jenny: Yes I do, for several reasons. I think it's been done so many times that people have lost trust in the process itself. They manipulate the process, and I don't believe they feel they can be honest anymore. Therefore, the results are skewed.

Bigger than that, change is happening in business and to people personally so much, that by the time you've done the survey, got in all the responses and spent three months navigating through the results, the whole world has shifted, from a business perspective and for you individually, since that moment when you filled in the survey. It might even just be that you had a bad train trip into work or whatever, but that one thing will have defined the moment. So by the time the results come in, they're already outdated.

I think we should be moving towards sentiment analysis and touch-points that show the business has its finger on the pulse much more than a survey could ever, ever do. On the other hand, it might be interesting to do an engagement survey here – an experiment to see how it works in a place that's never been used to it before!

Annabel: How do you measure the impact of IC? How do you know what 'good' looks like and whether you're doing a good job?

Jenny: I know it's probably not helpful to say in terms of defining best practice, but a lot of it comes down to experience and instinct, and just making sure you're not measuring for measuring's sake. I've been to quite a lot of events and conferences where people get up and talk about the dashboard they've got, and how many clicks they get on their intranet – and I'm not really interested in that kind of analysis.

What I *am* interested in is people's appreciation of the message, and how that makes them feel. So it comes back to using things like Yammer discussion boards and really getting a feel for people's understanding of the messages that they've heard. That's where I think IC can have its biggest impact because if it starts to learn how people are responding to sets or types of messages, the tone of voice, and the topics themselves, you can then form your communication strategy much more intelligently, based on what the audience is actually receiving.

Ear to the ground

In the light of her comments on the value of listening and reacting, we asked Jenny how effective the business is at adapting to employee feedback, particularly when that feedback is enriched by a Yammer-style environment. She explained that it's a matter of balance. It's just as easy to rush to judgemental reactions on internal social media – ah, who knew? – as it is in the rough and tumble of the Twittersphere, and the business must eschew the judgement trap in favour of listening, taking the temperature, and allowing the discussion to self-regulate. We can see how that takes a brave, discretely firm hand on the IC tiller, and have all the more respect for Jenny's quiet confidence that the company is getting there, although it is by no means perfect. Ultimately, she told us, the business should be empowering employees to make changes for themselves and avoiding a culture in which a leader's knee-jerk response to a piece of feedback is to dive in and apply his or her own fix.

Jenny raised an interesting possibility: that in the UK, particularly, our obsession with employee engagement and the annual survey has in fact created something of an 'entitlement culture'. Businesses are driven by responding to employee feedback all the time, and employees have bought in to the idea that the more they ask for, the more they will get. It's a cycle that is overdue for a bit of disruption. She certainly wasn't suggesting that the business doesn't have a duty to listen to employee feedback and enact big changes if required; but a culture, led from the top, in which employees are empowered to resolve smaller issues as they arise will provide a more dynamic environment for engagement. We got a stronger sense than ever that Jenny was speaking from the heart here – and with the full weight of her two decades' experience in comms.

Annabel: Here's a more personal question, then: what do you love about your role in IC?

Jenny: Everything. Well, I wouldn't have been doing it for so long if I didn't love it. I love the variety of it, the fact that I could be working on strategy with our CEO and the exec team one day, through to, I don't know, organizing tea and cakes because we just want to do something nice for our people.

The extent of things that you get involved in is huge, and then seeing the impact of your role is very exciting to me. For example, we recently ran a two-day executive and leadership event. By the end of Tuesday, there was such a buzz from having delivered something like that – influencing people by getting the team leaders to talk about the merger.

Annabel: How does IC fit in your organization today?

Jenny: Internal communication is part of the Chief Operating Officer's remit, which includes customer operations and HR. So I think it's quite well positioned from an influencing perspective. I worked in pretty much every area of a business over the years; corporate affairs, marketing, HR... It doesn't really matter where you report, as a good IC practitioner should be well versed at connecting the dots and building relationships right across a business no matter where they sit, as that's what the job entails.

Annabel: What are your top three tips for anyone who is looking to rise through the ranks as an effective IC practitioner?

Jenny: My number one tip is, if you're starting out in your career, don't get too hung up on having lots of direct contact with the CEO or senior leaders to begin with. Be careful what you wish for! There's plenty to be done in terms of influencing other people who have key roles in the organization – sometimes people can overlook that. It doesn't always have to be about the CEO. The Transformation Programme Director or the HR Director also have a lot of influence. In an ideal world, we think everything needs to come from the CEO but I just haven't found that to always be the reality. Instead, focus on working with what you've got.

The second top tip would be, don't try to control everything. If I go back over two decades ago when I started in communications, it was all about control. We were almost trained to take control. How many times have you heard the phrase Air Traffic 'Control' – I don't think we ever had control even when we thought we did! Instead, try to be a facilitator of the conversations and start the important discussions – even if it becomes controversial at times – allow employees to have a voice and drive their own conversations and outcomes. Too many people think they can control everything and with the budgets that we have today, it just isn't viable. You might as well set yourself up to fail. Social media channels are a wonderful gift that we should embrace.

My third top tip would be, practise what you preach. Too many times I've come across people who have worked in my team or I've communicated with who aren't prepared to take their own advice when they move into leadership roles. I remember one occasion when I was helping a senior colleague with an investor presentation she was going to give at an event. I sat there giving this woman, who had a huge amount of experience, advice about how to behave on stage and elevate her voice. And I thought, 'I shouldn't be telling anyone how to do this if I can't do it myself.' So I forced myself to speak at an event in front of 1,000 people. I did it really badly, and obviously I've since taught myself to get better at it. You've got to have credibility when you're communicating.

Can I have another tip? We can call it 3.1 if you like. Know how the business runs and know how the commercial side operates. I've seen many internal communicators fail because they don't have the credibility this generates. When you are talking to the CEO about results, for example, you have to know this stuff inside out. Otherwise all the great work we've done in getting IC to become a profession will be eroded because we'll be back to seeing it as this slightly aloof function on the side, rather than core to the business. Know your numbers as well as your words!

Transformative times

For her parting shot, Jenny returned to one of her big themes: the transformative effect of millennials and new technology on IC. She suggested that we are at a key moment in its evolution, and we probably don't yet truly understand what this means for IC. How can we, when the wider world probably hasn't come to terms with such rapid changes itself? With social media, there is a sense that its use is getting out of control. The fact is, it has already had a profound impact on IC, and it feeds into the hard-learnt lesson that internal communications need to feel and be authentic, without seeming to come from a specific IC 'machine'. People have long since wised up to any sense of comms-by-numbers. They will instantly see through anything that is heavily scripted or just too corporate in tone, or doesn't speak to them in plain English. That's why Jenny thinks leaders should be encouraged to get on Twitter and Yammer, where they can just be themselves and basically, be more 'real' to internal audiences.

That can be scary for some of us, because it means relinquishing a certain degree of control over perception and response. In essence, it means being brave, but we have to go with the rolling news culture we now live in, which is more fluid and faster than ever. It has changed people's expectations about the speed and volume of communication. Even the big broadcasters take risks with breaking stories, announcing them before they know all the details. A story will often be half-baked, and the broadcaster will occasionally be caught out and get things wrong, but the audience is there, demanding a snapshot of things as they are right here, right now. Jenny told us that the business world must buy into that model of information shared quickly – even when we don't necessarily know all the answers.

Given that in so many ways IC is in this fascinating state of flux, we wanted Jenny to tell us where she thinks it will be in 10 years' time. Unsurprisingly, she doesn't expect the function to be built around regular messages from the CEO. Nor does she predict a world of heavily scripted missives from leaders. Instead, she thinks the need for internal communicators will be founded more specifically on making sure channels are in place that empower other people to run their communications themselves: the previously mentioned role of the conversation facilitator will shift into sharper focus. This move towards connecting with the business and supporting people through collaboration has already started, and will become even more profound and important. Effectively, said Jenny, IC will be about bringing the external world into the business, through technology and new social platforms. That external stimulus will nourish and inspire innovation. It's a brave vision indeed, and one we would heartily commend – making it all the more frustrating that we can only continue to watch this space while we wait to see the extent to which it is ultimately realized!

The Institute of Internal Communication

08

How a professional body is leading the way in setting 21st century standards for excellence in internal communications and the importance of driving change from the inside

SUZANNE PECK

President, Institute of Internal Communication; Vice President, European Association for Internal Communication (FEIEA); Managing Director, The Sequel Group

Corporate purpose, a two-headed monster that complicates communications internally, tipping the delicate balance between an engaged workforce feeling valued, and the constant business pressure to focus on finance and performance. This startling image is not ours. It was conjured up by Suzanne Peck as she defined the challenges of sustaining vision during transitional times, and we were struck by this metaphor, which seemed to sum up the duality of the IC function as it exists today.

Uniquely among our interview subjects for this book, Suzanne wears two hats. She is MD of internal communication agency The Sequel Group, and President of the Institute of Internal Communication

(IoIC), an organization in which she has been active for more than 27 years. So when she uses the word 'schizophrenic' – emphatically not in any medical sense – to describe many companies' approach to delivering consistent messages on corporate purpose, she is speaking with a wealth of experience and observation at close quarters. Her philosophy, she explained to us, is that communicators should be encouraged to be curious within their organizations, to get involved and help to drive change from the inside rather than being a spectator on the outside.

Firmness of purpose

It quickly became obvious during our interview that this robust perspective informs her vision and predictions for the evolution of IC, and the need for change. Sometimes, she told us, an organization's approach to change is based on knee-jerk reactions rather than a planned strategy. Suzanne illustrated her point with a recent example of a company merger announcement in the press that was also news to the internal comms team. This does not fit well with a corporate purpose of 'building trust and keeping our people informed'. It epitomizes a corporate failure to understand the key role that employees can play as brand advocates and ambassadors.

Vision and purpose statements such as 'Our people are our greatest asset' or 'Our brand is our people' often conflict with business needs that ask those same people to work longer hours and do more for less without keeping them informed or articulating the 'Why?' effectively. That's where Suzanne's metaphor of a two-headed monster rears its scaly head.

Annabel: How would you say that IC is viewed as a profession today?

Suzanne: Very differently from how it was three decades ago: my own experience was that IC then was viewed as just the staff newspaper. We were officially part of marketing, but HR thought we should be answerable to them as well, so we didn't really have a home. Now, IC is increasingly seen as a function in its own right, and really adding value to an organization. It's an integral part of engaging employees with the business and helping them to do their jobs so that the company improves its business performance.

Annabel: What about 10 or 15 years down the line – how do you think it will be seen by then?

Suzanne: I don't think there will be an actual internal comms function. IC will just be something natural that business does. Although the function itself may not exist, the role of the internal communicator will still be important, because there needs to be an expert, a facilitator to bring people together, to be the connector and to challenge leadership about the messages they are sending. It's no longer about the creation and delivery of the message. It's more about the curating of that content, and making sure the right message goes to the right people at the right time.

Annabel: Can you describe some of the changes you've seen in terms of technology and channels?

Suzanne: Going back to early days, I remember when the fax was quite revolutionary and the wonder of first using e-mail! I think e-mail has made one of the biggest differences because many people feel that once they've sent an e-mail, they've communicated and that the job is done. I'm seeing in my industry almost a backlash against e-mail as a way of communicating.

There's also a shift from, say, two or three years ago, when it was all about the technology. The shininess has worn off a little bit and it's more about using the right tools for you and your organization. If you are a company with frontline staff, technology alone is not always going to help you reach them. Technology has opened up choices for audiences, but it's also forced internal communicators to think harder and smarter about how to use it to engage people.

One area that I don't feel will ever change – and quite rightly – is face-to-face communication. There's just no better way to communicate. In all the research and all the polls, it's the one thing that audiences say they want more of: face-to-face communication – give me time with my manager so that we can talk about my performance, my issues, and let my manager explain what's happening in the business and give me the context.

Blurred boundaries

By this stage in our arc of interviews, it was becoming clear that there is a widely shared view among IC practitioners that the traditional boundary between internal and external comms is blurring and may, eventually, vanish altogether. However, the spectre of increased regulation within many industries and the need for transparency are two potential flies in the ointment that could have a direct impact on how this vision pans out. Suzanne suggests that it spells the end of a 'rose-tinted' time in IC, when it was enough for messages to go through regular approval processes because there was a sense that they were 'only' going to an internal audience. Now, there is an increasing need for organizations to run internal communications through Compliance and Legal departments before they are transmitted. This presents a challenge for communicators as there's a delicate balance between what is legally 'allowable' and questioning the journalistic or creative integrity of the communication.

Suzanne was open to the view that internal and external comms should become a single function, and that this may well be the natural conclusion of a process that has been under way for many years. External and internal communication working together has to be a positive move. Although they may still need a slightly different stance or call to action, the content and spirit will be largely the same. The skill of the IC practitioner lies in adjusting the tone for the audience and channel. It's a subtle balance and something PR and marketing should also acknowledge rather than applying a sweeping tone for internal and external purposes. This brings us neatly to another regular and increasingly dominant theme: the role of millennials in influencing new definitions of IC in today's corporate environments.

Annabel: How are you managing the impact of millennials in the workplace?

Suzanne: Millennials bring an interesting set of challenges. I'm all for 'always on' accessible communication, and for caring that the business they're working for is a good company – internally and on the outside. But I personally have an issue with focusing so much on 'meeting the needs' of millennials and how organizations are going to attract and retain them. Yes, it's important to have this talent for the future, but there's a whole swathe of generations within organizations who also need nurturing because that's where the knowledge and the experience is. I hate to hear organizations talking about attracting the 'talented' people, playing to the geek scene and making everything whizzy, while forgetting that probably 80 per cent of their employees are multi-generational – and also talented and knowledgeable.

What would be ideal would be to fully understand the needs and challenges for each generation, and then to use that information to encourage closer working relationships, sharing of knowledge and collaboration: buddying up, exchanging information, mentoring the millennials with, say, baby boomers so they can each learn from each other.

Annabel: Do you believe the annual employee engagement survey is dead?

Suzanne: Yes. When I worked in-house in comms, we used to run an annual survey. Most of the responses would depend on people's experiences in the fortnight, the week or even the day before we carried it out. There was one survey in particular when, I think, we ran out of tea or coffee the month before. Our score for facilities in the office went right down! Everything would have been fine for the other 11 months! An annual survey, any survey, is just a snapshot in time. If we only check the temperature once a year, the danger is that what has gone immediately before could skew the results or the perceptions of that survey, and then the actions we take.

Annabel: What are your recommendations for companies that want to understand how their workers feel, or their levels of engagement?

Suzanne: Survey little and often. There's such apathy around annual surveys, especially the big 40-question ones. You need to set aside time with a strong cup of coffee before you can start. People are just too busy and they lose the will to live. By the time you get to question 15 you're desperate just to finish it, so the quality of response isn't there. For me, smaller and more frequent engagement gives you a better quality of feedback. It's more relevant, more valuable, less onerous and it's less demanding of people and their time.

Annabel: Can you describe best practices you've seen amongst some of your clients and how they measure IC?

Suzanne: I'm really interested in what Nationwide is doing at the moment, and that's because so many organizations would rather talk about engagement and communication than starting the conversation at the top. At Nationwide, it really is starting with the leadership team. They're out and about, talking to people. There's plenty of opportunity for people to share their views and feedback, and we're seeing employees valuing that. As a business, it is demonstrating leadership in practice, being open and transparent, inviting its people to talk to it about any issues. In one recent campaign, it saw terrific stats on engagement because there was a clear objective, a clear timeline and people understood the 'Why?' all along, and what they needed to do. It was simple. That's the key message: don't over complicate things – bring it to life and make it relevant to the audience.

Annabel: Did that involve face-to-face feedback or were there other channels?

Suzanne: It was a mixture. As each phase of the campaign went out, the impact was measured. We used the principle of asking just a few questions, from a trusted source and to a few people each time. Line managers sent it out so it wasn't from an anonymous e-mail address, and they selected a certain number of recipients within each department. Everyone understood the role they were playing in the bigger picture.

The wealth of experience

This attention to detail and a clear view of where the impetus for IC should come from are rooted in Suzanne's years of experience. Her profound belief in the integrated value of IC – when it is done properly – is based on accumulated wisdom (her own and from working with leading clients), which gives her perspective consider-able gravitas.

As she explained, the IoIC itself has a legacy of 65 years of busi-ness communication. The first half-century was relatively quiet, but the pace of change has quickened considerably during the last decade, as has demand for its services. As a not-for-profit organiza-tion, there are no vested or commercial interests to satisfy. Its sole mission is to promote best practice and excellence in IC. Suzanne takes great pride in its reputation for bringing practitioners together, and the wider reach it now has. For example, it runs foundation and advanced diploma courses, which provide recognized qualifications and standards in IC and a CPD programme. For Suzanne, this type of personal development, which requires commitment, is better than half-day workshops or two-day training programmes in which you get a certificate that isn't really proving anything. In a world that is connected 24/7 and with new people entering the industry, of course there's more that can be achieved, but IoIC's vision to drive standards and professionalism is making great strides forward.

Annabel: Would you say that companies that do take their employ-ees' feedback act on it?

Suzanne: Not always, no. I've just had a conversation with a client about the annual survey, and who 'owns' the actions. If it's just HR, or down to just IC, you're not going to be able to achieve very much. A lot depends on an organization's culture, and my personal view is that it starts – and ends – with line managers. They're the people with relationships and leadership. They're the individuals who can have a tangible and direct impact on employees in helping to change behaviour.

Annabel: What obstacles prevent this from happening in some companies?

Suzanne: If you make it complicated, it's going to be harder to do. The best example I have seen used a very simple dashboard of the key 20 or so actions from a quarterly survey. Then they prioritized each into red, amber or green so there were clear timelines and it was broken down into small, achievable chunks. And they had a successful outcome. It's the same as any project. Be clear and don't try to bite the whole apple at one time. Take small bites, get some results and then move on to the next bite.

Annabel: What are your top three tips for inspiring anybody who wants to work in IC?

Suzanne: Keep learning! Go on training courses, search the internet for useful blogs or sites and keep up to date with what's happening in the industry. Communication is a broad area so find the niche – the bit that you love. Decide what you want to be famous for! Then ensure you have the core skills to deliver and achieve, whether it's writing, design, strategy, management, culture, digital; whatever.

The second bit of advice I would suggest is to network. Talk to people doing similar jobs to you; go and spend time in marketing, in brand, in IT, anywhere that you can see how your job and theirs might dovetail, so that you understand their challenges and issues. Just contact people. If you ask, they are usually very flattered and happy to help.

Finally, don't think you want to work in comms because you want to be a writer or write a novel. It's a totally different skill set. You need to like people, to be interested in people, and you have to be able to listen. We have two eyes, two ears and one mouth for a very good reason and we should use them in equal proportion. Have an enquiring mind. Be inquisitive and curious. Be the eyes and ears in your organization and ask questions.

Annabel: And where do you find your inspiration?

Suzanne: I like *Harvard Business Review* – which makes me sound far more intellectual than I actually am – because it always makes me think about things I may never have considered! I like the way it takes a topic and brings together all the thinking around it in a clear and understandable way. I also admire the way the Royal Society of Arts does the same, bringing in thinking from different angles. Then there are things like Simply Communicate and the *Huffington Post*. For me, it's all about keeping an open mind. My children are now both at university and I find them inspiring for they are just constantly taking in information, changing their views in a considered way – being open. Talking to them about, say, how they use Snapchat and Instagram to communicate is fascinating: understanding how those channels work just 'in the moment', and then the message is gone but still understood.

Challenging roles

Suzanne told us that she believes the best internal communicators are people who are prepared to challenge, who aren't afraid to question why a business is taking a certain course of action. These are the practitioners who, in her book, add real value to the organization rather than working each day with blinkers firmly in place. The IC world seen through Suzanne's eyes is a dynamic place in which experience, the brave and the new can really work together to capture the corporate imagination. She is a self-confessed IC evangelist who never expected when she began work in internal comms many years ago that she would still be learning so many new things today. Her core journalism skills and IC experience are essential, but are influenced by fresh thinking, technology and the changing, increasingly digital, workplace. When she told us that she feels excited to be in comms right now, and that in fact there has never been a more interesting time for IC, it sounded like a tremendous rallying cry for practitioners at every stage of their own journey and experience. It is one we are equally excited to share.

April Six

09

How team building and connected leadership are helping a service business to go global without losing sight of core values that are being driven from the very top

FIONA SHEPHERD

CEO, April Six

An organization can only ever be as good as the people who work for it. This simple, fundamental and frequently overlooked observation was made by Fiona Shepherd at the very beginning of our conversation. As CEO of global marketing agency April Six (the name comes from the date it was established in 2000; following the acquisition of Proof Communication in 2014 it became April Six Proof) Fiona was speaking specifically about the challenges of IC from the perspective of a services business, but it's a truth that applies to any kind of company. Whatever you provide for your clients, it always comes back to the people who build and develop products, who grow your market, who engage your customers and forge relationships. Without them, you don't have a business. Fiona's point is that if you are selling something intangible and you don't have an actual commodity, the need to remain engaged with your employees is even more purely distilled. They need to come on the journey with you and tell the stories that will bring your services to life for your clients.

Keeping focus

After 16 years at the helm of April Six, Fiona has taken her people on a considerable journey of expansion. With its focus on the high-tech industry, the company has been honed by the pressures of quarterly budget cycles. It is, Fiona explained, completely tuned in to the primacy of the demand funnel and pipeline. The challenge is to maintain that focus as the business consolidates its global presence while it continues to enjoy micro-growth within each country of operation. One solution, it transpired, is to build a set of 'Tiger Teams'.

Imogen: What are the key things that drive your focus on internal comms?

Fiona: The first is the fact that we only have people and we are only as good as the people that we have working for us. I think the challenge for me and the deeper need for focus on it, has come as we have moved to be in three continents. We now have more than one agency, more than one capability and more than one location here in the United Kingdom. It becomes so much more difficult than being in one office and walking in every day when you can ask everybody how they are feeling. In the past, it was me walking into the agency: walking around and talking to people. There was no need to make it too formal. The reason we now have a serious focus on IC is that the shape of the business has changed, so we now need a definitive focus on employee communications.

Now, we're just about relaunching the brand – and brand values are nothing if you don't bring them to life through IC, which is where the focus and the creation of the 'Tiger Teams' comes from. This has become crucial. The Pulse Check™ and the Tiger Teams are the first steps towards it.

Imogen: Tell us more about the Tiger Teams!

Fiona: One of my beliefs is that if change from an employee perspective doesn't happen from within, it doesn't happen at all. I don't think you can dictate employee change. I don't think you can legislate it, and I don't think you can necessarily dictate from on high what people will or won't believe. So one of the interesting things for me has been to work out how we create employee engagement from within the businesses, especially across the different locations.

The Tiger Teams were created around two areas: employee retention and engagement, and corporate social responsibility (CSR), both of which are related. They work directly with me and there is a representative from each location on each Tiger Team. They become the ambassador for their team within their location, and they have played a fundamental role in shaping the Pulse Check™, executing it and now acting on the pillars of change that we've identified.

Imogen: How is the CSR aspect of your IC strategy taking shape?

Fiona: You have a strong sense of humanity in a people business. Every business is a person, isn't it? It has a personality, it has a soul. Even when you're global, there is still a significant amount of that – and it's consistent across all your locations. You should be able to go around a bigger organization and feel very similar things, sense that the core values are inherently the same. When we recruit as we expand, we are looking for the same common values, which means CSR is an important parameter for people's working environment here. Put another way, our culture is quite socially aware. I am very socially aware. It motivates me. I think we can get the company to be that way today by making people feel connected and motivated around specific sentiments and good causes. Individually you can have an impact but with CSR you can unite and collaborate to change things and really make a difference. So the Tiger Team has decided to create initiatives around a single purpose for our charities worldwide, which this year is to focus on homelessness. The company is giving every employee one day to go and do voluntary work, to take part and make a difference. We're also running a scheme called 'Better Futures', which is about affecting a hundred lives.

Of course one of the challenges is always how you balance the client work against this. One of the other reasons for putting the Tiger Teams in place is to stop it becoming yet another corporate idea that doesn't ever happen. I do think we'll actually achieve far more this way, and the Tiger Teams are the key to success. There's an overlap between CSR and employee engagement because the key to retaining people and making them feel engaged is to have strong corporate ethics. To behave in a socially conscious way, and to make people feel there is a culture here that is about caring and respect for others, is incredibly important. It trickles down into the sense of openness and humanity that you want to create in your employee brand.

Tiger power

Concepts and initiatives have flowed thick and fast from the Tiger Teams, which have already started to execute some of the ideas triggered by the Pulse Check™ results. Fiona outlined one of these, a buddy system, which provides new recruits with a buddy and a mentor to ease them into April Six over their first three months of employment. It has been implemented globally. The buddy, usually from a different discipline, offers friendly advice and guidance. The mentor, usually with the same capability set as the recruit, helps the new employee to build confidence as he or she assumes the role and responsibilities of the job.

Get connected

Fiona's hands-on approach to IC is also embodied in the 'Next Generation' club, which is for every employee in their first year of life with the agency. Wherever they are in the world, she will meet with them every couple of months for a 'Next Gen' session. The aim, she explained to us, is to create a layer of interaction and connectivity among new and recent employees, which helps them to engage with longer-serving colleagues.

It was fascinating to hear Fiona describe the subtle tensions within a 16-year-old business: there are layers of staff who have been there long enough to form a 'family', which can be difficult for new people to feel part of, especially when there is a strong, well-evolved culture.

If you've been working in that culture for 16 years, she explained, you've probably stopped thinking about it, you've simply become an intrinsic part of it – and that's a resource worth tapping into.

Strategies like 'Next Generation' help to reinforce a support structure, creating an organization without boundaries or silos. Connections are not defined by disciplines or roles, but by the shared experience of being employed by the organization. The expected outcome, she said, is that the business ends up with a constantly refreshed team, empowered to create its own support structure and network, which in turn help it to grow up within the organization. Crucially, because Fiona is leading the strategy, new arrivals will also stay connected with her from the start, giving her a way to make sure she feels connected herself, and a vehicle to share her vision and passion for the business with everyone who joins.

Imogen: How have all these initiatives made you think about leadership, particularly the role of the CEO?

Fiona: I think leadership apart, when you talk about employee communications, retention and engagement, you're talking about it at every level, and that's part of the challenge. You have to think about it across the whole of the business. As a CEO, you have the responsibility to share your vision at different levels and depths across the organization. If you bring it to the very top of the organization, and you look at the executive leadership team and the local board level teams, you need to keep them connected to that vision. By keeping them connected, everyone can be encouraged to create new initiatives or revive old ones.

For example, we're just about to relaunch the April Six Academy, which is an internal training academy. The leadership team gets together for a week twice a year and builds vision and strategies collaboratively. At the time of speaking, the next one will mark the start of their leadership training, with a facilitated training day, team building and one-to-one mentoring. Most of them have already been on the Leadership Training 101 sessions, which is a three-month course. The academy is about moving up to the next level by creating a single team of leaders that are on the journey together. We'll be investing in moving forward in a connected fashion because, again, it's important to create that single agency vision worldwide, with everyone on the same page. I think it will encourage them to have the same attitude to all their people, and that will strengthen broader employee engagement. Training is a part of employee retention and engagement but it also benefits the business. It should lead to a tangible, seismic change in the way individuals work together, collaborate, and the way in which they feel empowered to take on their role.

I also think there must be some mindfulness. I don't want to be a CEO who only thinks about the numbers. At the end of the day, if your organization is firing on all cylinders, the numbers will happen anyway. So, my focus is less on the numbers now and more on the people. The more I empower them, the more successful we'll be anyway.

Imogen: How are you finding the arrival of millennials in the workplace?

Fiona: We are absolutely loving them. We have a big focus on graduates and interns anyway, with an ongoing graduate programme. I think we've got between five and 10 graduates at the moment in the business. The interesting thing for me is that the world is changing radically – and they are the ones helping us to stay abreast of it. We find them refreshing. Some people might find them difficult because they work in a different way, but if you've had teenage kids or have millennial children, which I do, you have to adapt to engage with them anyway. You have to alter the way you plan and the way you think with millennials. Outside work, the way in which I communicate with my kids is completely different to the way my parents communicated with me. I've had to shift my understanding of how they judge a situation or their expectations. I am forever entirely frustrated by their lack of patience! But I live with it at home and I live with it at work. If you don't work with it, you can't get the best from it.

You can either fight it or understand they are a product of their generation: a product of the technology they live with and the way in which they've been taught. I mean, my son is now 25 per cent taught on an iPad at school. So I can't expect people to come here and work the way that I worked a long time ago. We are embracing it and changing because of it. You can either love what they bring to the workplace or you can be afraid of it. If we are to stay current, we have to love it and get excited about the challenges they bring to us. I think their energy levels are immense. But I also think you have to recruit well.

Attention to detail

Fiona's point about careful recruitment almost sounded like an afterthought, but we urged her to consider it in more detail because throughout these interviews, the challenges and fluidity of the recruitment market in all sectors has been an abiding theme. The opportunity to capture the view from someone who, in building a successful and dynamic global business for 16 years, has inevitably navigated several changes in the recruitment tides, was too good to miss.

She didn't hold back. You need well-informed people with contextual awareness of influences beyond the business itself, she insisted. If they combine that with a little experience – of life and work – and evidence of their ability to apply themselves, you are looking at likely candidates. They probably already appreciate how difficult it is to get internships and summer jobs, because they've been there and done that, and they bring the experience with them. They will respond positively to clear internal messages about what they're going to be doing. It's a matter of keeping their ambitions realistic, timely and long term, so they don't expect to be writing Microsoft strategy next week or even next year.

Spot the intern

As Fiona reminded us, a lot of millennials do come out thinking that they're ready to take on the world – but we all know the journey is not quite that intense or immediate. April Six sets expectations well and, thanks to the buddy system, it also embraces and treats new people like normal, stakeholding members of the team from the start.

Fiona is adamant that we wouldn't be able to walk into the office and point out the interns. That's different from the typical internship experience which, too often, leaves people feeling second-class. Her message is that they're in, part of the team, and delivering from day one. She thinks that helps them to feel valued, and that they can grow their career at April Six; in short, they want to stay there. Millennials, she admitted, seem to have a deep need to keep moving: if you're not careful, you can lose them almost as quickly as you found them.

She cited April Six's UK head of planning, who joined the company 10 years ago, as an example of successful graduate recruitment. The last thing you want is for your talent to think it's got to move around constantly to get anywhere, which is where great, clear IC comes in, through engagement: doing full appraisals every year, mapping out people's growth potential, as well as quarterly views so you can spot areas for personal growth. Too often in an organization, she told us, there is a lack of clarity around what an employee needs to do to get to the next level.

At April Six, through a combination of the training academy and the appraisal system, the map is constantly refined and they are given every help with following it. It doesn't mean they always get there, but it means that they know what they've got to do to get there. In the end it comes down to effort – and with employee engagement, if you put the effort in, you'll get the return.

> **Imogen:** How have you managed to keep everything on track while there's been quite a lot of change at April Six?

> **Fiona:** It has been huge, opening the office in the United States (San Francisco) and then going global. One of the basic principles you need to understand is that nobody likes change. Well, they do like it, but only when they can understand it, embrace it and feel that it's good, that they're changing with the organization. Whether a period of immense change is based on setting up a new agency in the States or integrating the PR capability and going through an acquisition, it's still about realizing that as humans, what we want to do is to understand the change and our role in it. We need to understand how change is better for us personally, and for the organization as a whole.

I think the transparency we have here is enormous. We're open about everything. We have quarterly global all-hands calls where we do video conferencing room-to-room so that everybody can see each other. I tend to do it from a different location each quarter. I also think we are open about what those changes are, what they're going to mean to the organization in the long run. Any change is always going to have a period of effort before you get to the point of feeling the benefit. It's a bit like keeping faith, isn't it? No pain, no gain.

When we launched in the United States, we had to be the delivery arm for the San Francisco office here in the United Kingdom, while they become established. You could see that as a negative or positive thing in relation to your job, but we helped everyone to see it as a positive, so that people here understood how exciting it was going to be: what the opportunities would be for them when we had a global business and a fully functional US agency – which we do have now.

With the acquisition of Proof (April Six bought Proof Communication in 2014), there's another interesting dynamic. It was obviously a very successful acquisition and they are part of the family now – we're rebranded as April Six Proof. One of the ways to achieve a successful acquisition – and I think every CEO should think this through – is by ensuring that when a business is first acquired, every interaction they have with you is a positive one. You are not shackling them or slowing them down. You are adding value to what they do.

Imogen: Can you give me an example of that?

Fiona: Yes. The right acquisition strategy for us was to buy a successful company, which Proof was, rather than a broken one. They were growing. What they needed me to do was to help them to get the business to a point where it was even more successful, just as the Mission Group aimed to do for us (April Six is part of Mission's 13-strong portfolio of agencies), I've done with them – given them a fair amount of independence in the first year post-acquisition. I didn't need them to tell me how to do it, so I didn't try. I didn't interfere with Proof's business. What I tried to do was to help them think about what comes next and help them think about how being associated with April Six increased their opportunity, help them to interact with people and feel the benefit of being part of a greater talent pool. You do that gently, and you do it over time. Then you'll find people grow, and they genuinely want to be part of the relationship.

The value of choice

Here, Fiona drew an arresting analogy: it's embarking on an arranged marriage but still being given a chance to affect the decision. If an element of choice is still there, people can feel that they are, to an extent, electing to be part of the organization's destiny and are joining the party willingly. So when the day comes that you offer the name-change as a suggestion, everyone is more likely to see it as a positive idea rather than feeling that somebody just snatched away their original sense of purpose.

Fiona returned to her central theme of team-building, reiterating how connections are forged at every level of the business, and creating value-added environments because everyone is working together. As she put it to us, a successful acquisition is like an eccentric sum: one plus one must equal three – the two original entities become a dynamic, third organization. If it doesn't, she counselled, don't do it. Your focus should be on the three: what's the added value for employees across all of the businesses that makes it worth putting their energies and commitments into the journey?

You have to be really clear about what the journey is, so that nothing comes as a surprise. This maxim is currently being applied to the opening of the company's Singapore office, helping to make sure that everybody can see the purpose and the ultimate destination – and can have confidence in the leadership. Fiona likens herself to the captain of the ship. If everyone can see you setting a clear course from the helm, they'll follow. If not, unsettled feelings will be quick to rise.

Honesty is a core brand value at April Six. Mistakes per se don't matter the first time because they are part of personal and organizational growth – everyone learns from them, and the business gets bigger and better. Just don't keep making the same one! Above all, she said, keep excited about the company's goals and destination and make sure that clarity of vision is always at the heart of your messages. It turns out that there is still room for some more traditional IC tools in driving and informing that vision.

Imogen: Is the annual employee engagement survey dead?

Fiona: I think there's still a need for an annual one because if you look at KPIs and you look at big change, it's going to take a year to happen and impact. You want to be able to set a kind of foundation or measurement for improvement, and that's exactly what the annual survey does. The first one will set a benchmark, and then we want to see improvement on that, year on year, on year. It is certainly the most interesting one. There is nothing quite like asking everybody for their insights, and reacting to them.

Measuring employee sentiment is not a one-off annual task and that's partly what our Tiger Teams are about – taking a constant pulse within the agencies by talking to people in their individual locations. On top of that we are moving to quarterly checking around key points. There are specific pillars of change that the annual survey has established. We will pulse check around those pillars. If we've focused on one pillar in a quarter, we'll want to make sure we have generated the correct impact.

So I don't think the annual survey is dead. I think it's just as important as ever, and is the foundation for informed employee engagement – it's just not the only thing. You also need the constant focus from some sort of internal committee, which in our case is the Tiger Teams. If you work in an organization where once a year you stick your litmus paper in, take it out, and then do nothing, that will always yield disappointment. If you want people to give you their opinion, you have to be prepared to take the time and make the commitment to improving things around their commentary. They'll just lose interest if they don't see change as a result of their input.

Imogen: How do you plan to measure it, aside from benchmarking by asking the questions again?

Fiona: Through the strategic imperatives initiatives that have been created, and an internal activation plan based on the feedback. The real value will come from the initiatives that arise from the survey. It will be great to have the survey because it gives you a hard measurement of what you've achieved, but it's even more important to me that our surveys shape our internal programmes and that those initiatives will address multiple areas, in the same way that the buddy and mentoring scheme, the 'Next Generation' Club and the April Six Academy have all been born out of our pillars.

I don't think it's just about the metrics. Sure, the KPIs are measured against those metrics. But the organization changes as a result of the initiatives that you deliver as result of your discoveries. And for us, that will be the biggest fundamental value of it. We'll be realizing the benefits of the rigour and effort that we've put into the initiatives that underpin it.

Imogen: What have you loved about this process of change and engagement?

Fiona: Realizing that being worried that people wouldn't participate was a false concern and the fact that people cared and valued the initiative enough to take part. As CEO, what I've found most interesting is that, especially if you start to work across multiple locations and be slightly less engaged in the day-to-day, I now have a way of making sure that I can see inside the organization.

It's giving me an insight that I used to inherently have because I 'lived' amongst them all. It allows me to feel connected to and understand the business better. In all honesty, it comes back to one of my original points, which is that we are only about people. They are our most important asset. So this process has given me a framework to confidently think about how we will become 150 people, and then 200 people, without losing connectivity with the human aspect. I think it's going to help us to stay true to our brand values as well.

It also gives me a foundational layer to create initiatives around the brand values. So now I can ask, 'Ok – what are our five or six brand values? How do we make them feel real for our employees?

And can we get a sense of them understanding what they are?' Sometimes, as leaders, we get called into doing IC for people, and it can become more about volume than value. Our Tiger Team approach allows us to engage in the right way, with the right people, at the right time, and I love anything that is about people: whether it's from a CSR perspective and about people who need our help; or whether it's from an employee retention perspective and about the people we employ, and how we can create a workplace for them where they can work hard but feel valued and respected, and can see a future.

Directional certainty

Feeling confident about the direction of the business is certainly essential for any clear-thinking leader, even allowing for the ups and downs that are part of any organization's linear progression. Fiona developed this line of complexity by accentuating the value of employment engagement tools in managing the process of change, and providing the levels of insight that will give you that vital confidence. Every business will have its moments of predictability and unpredictability. You have to retain as much control as realistically possible while still allowing people to have a voice, and the more you measure, the more you can manage and keep your hand on the tiller, using the information delivered by measurement.

Fiona, it is utterly clear by now, values the fact that no matter where someone is in her organization, what their responsibility is, or how long they've been there, they all have an equal voice. This is no time for undue modesty, and she is quietly confident that a survey would reveal a core truth that has emerged from her 16 years at the helm, and which will be confirmed by long-timers on the April Six journey: that people's voices are more important to her than anything. If you're part of the company, you will have the ability to affect things and be heard: somebody who joined the business last week is no less important to its future – or indeed Fiona's – than somebody who joined five or 10 years ago. Longevity is important, but it's a different thing.

With April Six being part of the Mission Group, Fiona also has a broader role and opportunity to promote the values and opportunities of employee engagement. Each agency within the group naturally has its own style, approach and levels of engagement. Fiona suggested to us that April Six is one of those in which employee engagement has contributed significantly to success – and that experience gives her tangible justification for some of her strategic decisions: marketing budget is earned by demonstrable ROI and value, for example. She knows her fellow CEOs on the board of the Group want to see hard facts about the business's success. She gets immense satisfaction from not just paying lip service to the old maxim about employees and customers being at the centre of every decision. She provides evidence for the reality – and feels that adds credibility to some of the basic principles of her operational strategy for the organization.

This approach also gives her something hard on which to plan for the year ahead. It's never just based on gut feeling, but on real insight and intelligence. She thinks that only helps strengthen your credibility when you take it to a higher level and share your thinking about where the organization will be in five or 10 years' time: it's done with a real knowledge of what you have today. In Fiona's book, the world's better businesses are those that understand the inherent need to understand their people.

Imogen: In terms of your role today, what would be your tips for success?

Fiona: Know what you want to achieve. Know what your journey is and work with other really talented people. If you know where you want to go and you're surrounded by hugely talented people, I think you can only grow and learn. I grow and learn every day by connecting myself, and by being with people who stretch me. It doesn't matter how old or how senior you get. I just love being amongst talented people, whether they're 21 and just out of university or running a business.

Next, always work hard and with passion – or don't do it at all. I still ask myself when I go home every night, if I did justice to myself and my team. I ask myself, was April Six a better or more successful place today because of the things that I did? If the answer is no, then I'll probably have some work to do in the evening. For me, it's about did I guide well? Did I make good decisions? Was I clear about our directions and intentions? Did I support people, no matter their level, when they looked like they needed support?

Good parenting

Ending our interview with a series of questions turned out to be a provocative conclusion, not least because these are all questions that any self-respecting IC professionals should also be asking themselves as they make the journey home at the end of every working day. The answers won't always be black and white, and you won't always be able to say, in all honesty, 'Yes, absolutely!' But it ought at least to be the usual answer. If you can answer in the affirmative, it is probably a sign that, like Fiona, you strive to be conscious of what other people think. In her view, if you're going to lead, they need to look up to you and admire you. There's no room for having a bad day, publicly at least. She sets herself a pretty high standard: people have to see her and think that, whatever happens, as a leader she is calm, decisive, knows where she's going – and always energetic and passionate about what the business is doing. She urges other leaders to be the same, and inspire others as a result.

In short, she told us that no matter what disruptions have occurred outside, she will always come into the office and be the person April Six employees deserve in a leader. They trust her to do it. She threw one final analogy into the mix: it is, she said, like being a parent. Her responsibility is to be the best leader for them that she can be, and that means believing everything is possible, even if nothing is easy. You can do whatever you want, but understand that it's going to take 120 per cent of you to make it happen, no matter what it is. If you don't put in 120 per cent, then it won't happen. Of course you need to take everyone on that same journey – but without the effort, the destination will be a lot harder to reach.

Natural England   10

How strong story-telling, data
and insight are helping to confirm
IC as enabler, not mail box, at one
government agency

SHIONA ADAMSON

Head of Internal Communication and Communications Services,

Natural England

If there is one bone of contention to emerge from the interviews we carried out for this book, it is the annual employee engagement survey. Feelings about its current status are mixed indeed. For every practitioner who believes that it has long since run out of gas in this age of instant communication and reaction, there is another who reckons that with the right tweaks and modifications, it still has plenty to offer as an engagement measurement tool.

Even before we spoke, Shiona Adamson, Head of Internal Communication and Communications Services at Natural England, had placed herself firmly in the latter camp, quoting one of the fundamental rules of successful internal communications according to IC guru Liam FitzPatrick in her pre-interview Pulse Check™: 'Come with data, leave with respect.' FitzPatrick has pointed out that senior managers deal in facts and spreadsheets – information about process and outcomes, simply presented to enable their decision making (FitzPatrick and Valskov, 2014). If IC is to earn respect in the boardroom, data that shows its impact on the things that matter to the business is crucial and, carefully and properly conceived, the annual survey is a sure-fire way of generating that data. Shiona told us that survey data complements the equally valid, softer and more 'ear to the ground' or anecdotal aspect of IC – and that at a time when transparency is valued and strategically pursued, senior managers still need to know that the advice they are getting is based on science rather than hunch.

Winds of change

Natural England is a non-departmental public body, one of DEFRA's largest delivery agencies, and the UK Government's conservation adviser. Based in multiple locations around the country, Natural England works locally with partners on land and at sea to put people at the heart of the environment, guided by its ambition to redefine the idea of conservation in the public imagination. Natural England manages over half of the country's National Nature Reserves, is opening up the whole coastline around England for people to enjoy, and works closely with landowners to help them manage their land in ways that attract and enhance nature.

It is an interesting time to be part of an organization that occupies its own space in places throughout England – discrete from government and policy making, but facing the challenges of managing rapid change, dispersed staff and cost pressures in common with many government agencies. As we discovered, the impact of those demands on Natural England's IC strategy is significant.

Annabel: How would you say that internal comms is viewed as a profession today?

Shiona: While it will always depend to an extent on the experience and personalities of the senior team – the primary stakeholders of internal communication – there are countless examples and case studies that show that IC can really help to deliver strategy and vision. It has grown as an enabler, of strategic delivery. If the people who work in your organization don't understand or act on the vision you've set out, you'll never be able to realize it. Communicating it internally and inspiring the people behind it is an essential lever and our senior team knows this.

Staff don't necessarily see IC as a service though. It's almost got to the point where they might take it for granted – just being able to say what they think, learn what's going on beyond their immediate team, hear what the organization is planning. However, if you took one of their channels away, like the intranet, messages from the senior team, or events to gather people together – some of the basic tactical things that we do – they would certainly notice. They would feel as if they were living in a bit of a vacuum.

If you're talking about how IC is viewed as a profession with recruitment potential, or for graduates or students who are considering a career in the world of business, I think maybe it still has a little way to go in terms of being recognized in the same way as, say, law or medicine. As one of the major disciplines within the overall communications mix, internal comms is increasingly showing how it contributes to business delivery and productivity.

Annabel: How does your organization keep sight of corporate purpose during a period of transition? Have you been in an IC role when your organization has been through a period of transition?

Shiona: In my career, many times, ranging from downsizing offices, through to mergers or acquisitions. I've worked in the public and private sectors. Sometimes it has basic financial or efficiency drivers. Sometimes there is a change in strategic direction as the organization itself matures. In each case, the key message or the premise of the change has centred on the purpose of the organization and why it needs to shift.

With something like office downsizing, which really affects people on a personal, immediate level, it's very difficult to keep reminding them of why this has to be done. But I've seen a progression of honesty or increased integrity in the way that the message is delivered. The word 'spin' is no longer really there. I think that's partly down to internal communicators encouraging senior leaders to be as open and honest as possible with employees about the reasons why an organization is changing. If the reason for downsizing an office estate is to save cost, and the alternative to moving offices is to reduce the number of people in the organization, that's sometimes the best message you can give.

At the moment within Natural England, the senior team has set out a vision, 'Towards 2020'. It's not simply a pretty mission statement of what we're going to be doing in 2020. It's an articulation of the drivers and the influences on our business, and the reasons *why* we need to change the way that we do business to fulfil our purpose of redefining the country's approach to conservation in the 21st century.

Conservation is dear to our people's hearts. That's why they joined the organization: to preserve and enhance nature. The message that the organization is giving is that we need to listen to the influences around us, particularly government, the priorities of the voters, the voices around the economy and the need to grow it, so that we can find the best ways for nature and the economy to work together. As we speak, it's National Park Week. Half the reason to visit our National Parks is of course to see the beautiful views and experience nature and bring your children, but we also need people to spend money when they visit because nature can't live in a vacuum. In order for nature to thrive or for people to value it, it must be able to exist alongside business and development. That message can be hard to get across for people who have grown up wanting to protect animals and plants. We've been gradually showing where it can happen, for example with the opening of our coastal path around England. This is done with a message of opening the coast up for access, for people to preserve and enhance nature, but also to connect people with the coastal towns where they can buy their lunches and spend their money.

Delivering on the 'Towards 2020' premise will require some behavioural change in people within the organization, and there is resistance to it. We have to start the conversation about what this might look like, without being too prescriptive about a mission statement that everyone is under orders to follow. We need to ask them for their ideas, drivers and influences.

We started with a series of 21 workshops led by our directors and area managers around the country, with input sessions from other staff. We used an impactful infographic showing the influences on Natural England, and opened up the discussion in plenary sessions where senior managers were subjected to quite good scrutiny, and questioned about why we're doing this – do we really need change when what we're already doing is quite good? Then we broke the discussion down into smaller groups, and the feedback we got from that was typical for the first stage of engagement around a new corporate direction: 'Thank you for coming to speak to me. I really enjoyed talking to the senior managers. It's been very thought-provoking, but I don't yet believe that what I said will be taken into account when it comes to determining the operational changes that need to take place.' It's the face-to-face contacts, offering people a voice in the changes, making it personal, making it informal, which is the classic way to engage people in Natural England: making them central to the way we deliver our vision, not by dumping it all in front of them and telling them what they need to do.

Sourcing apprentices

Interestingly, the millennials-related challenges being addressed by many of our IC practitioners are less prevalent at Natural England. Shiona said there is a noticeable shortfall of millennials entering the public sector compared with other industries, but this is likely to change. The government has made a huge investment in apprenticeship schemes, designed to encourage young people into the workplace, as well as building a more diverse intake by offering career-change prospects for people. Natural England aims to add 40 new apprentices to its 2,000-strong staff roster in the coming years. Shiona told us that the feedback from many of the apprentices who have already progressed through Natural England suggests the opportunity has been an epiphany for them.

Natural England prides itself on being open to new ideas and innovation, and has discovered that keen millennials have an ability to help everyone open up their minds and spot business opportunities that might not otherwise have occurred to them, even in the public sector, which is sometimes criticized for being a little slow to adopt the exciting technologies that have major millennial appeal. Here, Shiona observed, the government's focus on open data is also having an impact. Millennials get it. They understand the systems, software and technology required to make data open to citizens. That makes organizations such as Natural England increasingly attractive. It also means the organization will need to galvanize itself to manage them effectively as they increase their presence on the working landscape.

Annabel: Tell me about the challenges of managing millennials once they are in the workplace.

Shiona: I guess they're not necessarily working next to many of their peers. So, while it's appealing to learn from those who are older and more experienced than themselves, they might feel that they're not necessarily bouncing around ideas as part of a cohort, and as a result they can be slightly more solitary in terms of their thinking and behaviour.

One of the challenges is technology, but government is getting there. I'm sitting here with my work iPhone. We have good mobile technology, are on the brink of making it more widely available to colleagues out in the field and we use Enterprise Social Networks like Yammer. The government is not in the dark ages but internal communicators play a role as 'grit in the oyster' for digital technology, helping to create and sell in the business case that will allow people to communicate and collaborate with each other, regardless of location. We need to lead the way in introducing the technology that will benefit everybody – not just millennials.

Annabel: How about the softer skill side and their actual ability to integrate into a workforce with a wide age range?

Shiona: You need to make sure that you're recruiting people who have the soft skills as well as the technical skills to be able to function within an organization, but I don't think that organizations need to spend too much time thinking about how to especially attract millennials. Most companies have a great deal to offer young people and maybe just need to think about how they explain and position their offer – the employer brand, if you like. If it's attractive, it's attractive, and if you're drawn as a millennial towards working for an organization that protects the nature of the country, you're drawn regardless of how funky the technology is.

Annabel: How are increased regulation and the need for transparency affecting your organization?

Shiona: The government is accountable to the taxpayer. I think the trends in social media, which offer the public much more of a voice, plus the introduction of the Freedom of Information Act, have all increasingly put our actions under scrutiny by a diverse range of stakeholders. We are used to it.

A lot of emphasis is placed on codes of conduct and the impact of decisions – not just on budgets or the bottom line and its equivalents in the public sector, but on the impression that they will give to the public. We've already talked about openness and transparency between staff and senior management. It's the same between the government and its public.

I have seen one shift over the last couple of years: government spokespeople are increasingly confident about calling a spade a spade, being open and honest, because people will see through any spin. One of the main rules of good media relations is to apologize if you have done something wrong.

This is very much reflected in the world of IC. We are open to comment, open to criticism, and we haven't published ghost-written blogs at Natural England for several years now. The senior managers write in their own voices. People are warming to it and I've seen an organic increase of confidence in both the writers, because they are writing about what they believe in and know about, and the staff, who feel they can comment on the posts and know that leaders will listen and respond.

This said, we (the 'centre') have been accused of 'optimism Tourette's' recently! This shows a mismatch between what some people are feeling and how the organization projects itself at a corporate level. Ironically though, staff create 95 per cent of our corporate stories or content and my team acts more as a curator. Put simply, no two people think or feel the same so it's essential for the IC team to create safe spaces for people to share their wide-ranging views.

Data imperative

This was the point in our conversation when we asked Shiona if she believes the annual employee engagement survey is dead – and received a resounding 'No!' Data, she insisted, remains central to any senior manager's understanding of the impact of his or her decisions on the organization. She doesn't suggest the survey is a replacement for instinct or an instant poll. Sometimes, she told us, you just know that decisions are right or wrong based on your experience and gut instinct but, increasingly, that must be based on data, on evidence. Shiona praised the work of the Government Communication Service which, through its professional improvement programme, has been encouraging and supporting IC practitioners to bring insight to bear on the evidence and address the key question: what does the data really tell us about our audiences?

Of course this isn't limited to annual survey results. Focus groups can help to penetrate the numbers and discover how they actually translate in practice. In other words, data and insight combined create a powerful tool to help decision making, but an annual survey, she told us, is still a great way to consistently monitor trends and improvements. It's a platform from which you can drill down, using pulse surveys, conversations, focus groups and web analytics and carry out a real-time assessment of how the organization is feeling. The measurement of year-on-year improvement (or otherwise!) of employee engagement is still most efficiently achieved through an annual survey. Hearing Shiona talk about the accumulative, tiered gathering of information made us curious about how the impact of IC is gauged and assessed at Natural England.

Annabel: Do you measure the impact of internal communications, and if so how?

Shiona: Yes, we do. The Government Communication Service has really seen the need to support IC in terms of skills development by providing the tools to consistently measure, compare and share experience across government. Measuring impact is almost a drill now. We don't just measure what people thought of the lunch at an event. We measure the inputs versus the outputs, the 'out-takes', and outcomes for overall staff engagement. We measure the over-all outcome of engagement using five questions that make up an engagement 'index'. We've started doing this monthly on a sample basis to get a more immediate sense of where staff are.

I'm currently compiling a mid-year 'Impact and insights' report. It pulls in the data from various sources to inform how engaged the workforce is and brings in insight we've gathered from high-performing teams to show what influences the results. For example, the team with the highest engagement scores does lots of little thoughtful things to recognize individuals' contributions, like a personalized e-mail from their peers to say 'Thank you, well done, brilliant work' with a £50 voucher attached. Natural England's internal comms and engagement strategy and our reporting framework are built around what we call our operating model for internal communications, which is based on the four enablers of engagement success: strategic narrative, engaging managers, employee voice, and integrity.

We state the desired outcome around creating and telling the story of the organization and its purpose. We talk about all our inputs, such as how many intranet articles we've produced that seek to tell this story. We measure the outputs in terms of the number of page views, events held, and the number of people who are talking about us. We consider the out-takes, or how people felt about the events, and the sentiment around people's comments. We are basically mirroring what's always been done with media relations. Assessing the outcomes is where we need to apply our judgement: what is the actual engagement level, and how many people can express, in their own words, what the vision of the organization is? All of this funnels into the employee engagement index which, ultimately and hopefully, contributes to productivity.

We do that for each of the four enablers. So, strategic narrative (which we just call 'telling our story') is engaging managers, getting them to tell their story, assessing their skills and comms, looking at how their training went and its impact on the staff that they manage. For employee voice we used to just measure how many opportunities we have given to people, to attend an event for example; now we think about the actual outcomes. Integrity is more difficult to measure: the authenticity and tone of the IC voice and what's being communicated in the organization. I always explain that this is the extent to which people actually believe that what they are being told is true (the say-do gap), and the extent to which they would do something differently as a result of it. It's quite a soft thing to measure.

So where we can, we're trying to put hard evidence against something that was previously soft. It's done annually, backed up by more regular pulse surveys and dashboards, because it's the annual employee survey that tells us the ultimate outcome of the organization's investment in consciously communicating and engaging with employees. It's not perfect but I don't think that measurement of human behaviour is easy.

There are a huge number of resources which the Government Communication Service has created to help with evaluation and other important aspects of the discipline. It's free and available to all communications practitioners via https://gcs.civilservice.gov.uk/ and for internal communicators specifically, we've created the IC Space, https://communication.cabinetoffice.gov.uk/ic-space/ which gets great feedback internationally for the way in which the IC community across government is creating and sharing expertise across all sectors.

Annabel: What about acting on the employee feedback? How effective are you at acting on it?

Shiona: One shift that we've seen recently was driven by our CEO, to set up working groups of staff to look at key themes that came through in the employee survey. I'm sure it's still the same in lots of organizations: you have the annual employee survey, then you set up small working groups to act team by team on the results and really think about what they mean for each team. It's different from how we've done this before because these working groups are totally empowered to make recommendations to the senior team, that are generally all taken on board and implemented.

One recent example of how we act on feedback is the different approach we're taking to reward and recognition. Employee voice is not just the extent to which you feel you can say what you think about an organization; it's the extent to which you feel recognized and rewarded for working in the right direction. The results of the last employee survey were not so positive about this. So the CEO empowered several groups of staff to really think about it, analyse what it meant in practice, and come up with ideas and suggestions for changing the way that we reward and recognize people.

Another example of acting on feedback, which has had quite a lot of impact, is that we revisited the way we give small token rewards to thank people for discretionary effort – for going above and beyond their normal call of duty. It used to be £25 per person, or you could reward a team to say thank you. Obviously, as a public body we are answerable to the taxpayer for the way that we do this, hence the small sum. Feedback from one of the working groups suggested that if we were to double the amount to £50, it would make a big difference. So we found the budget to do this.

All this indicates a slightly different approach, where the staff themselves have been empowered to analyse why something might not be good, and make suggestions. I think that without exception, all these gestures were agreed and acted on by the senior team.

High network benefits

Adding to a voice of unanimity that emerged across all our interviews, Shiona told us that the sheer variety – and, if we're honest, the unpredictability – of touch-points and challenges is one of the main attractions for the professional IC practitioner. It does not, she explained, make her a jack-of-all-trades, but it does mean that she has a good reason to have a finger in lots of different pies. It also means she knows a lot of people throughout the organization – and a little about a lot that's going on, as a result! Just being able to tap into that network by picking up the phone or sending an instant message means that she can instantly delve a bit deeper into some basic results or find out more about a rumour that she has heard.

It struck us that this natural curiosity is one of the IC practitioner's most important tools, combined with the ability to interpret snippets and hints of information and pursue them with the right question: a kind of professional sixth sense, which is fed constantly by a wider, unofficial comms network. It is something that is enabled by experience – but as Shiona believes, is supplementary to the other evidence gathered through employee surveys and other sources.

Shiona is also inspired by the drive from the Government Communication Service to professionalize and create standards for IC, making sure that it is never simply an attempt to reinvent the wheel. She is excited to participate in programmes such as 'Leaders as communicators', which are now being rolled out across government to help improve the communications abilities of line managers. She clearly feels that it's a privilege to be part of the designing and rolling out of these programmes, which are a collegiate and collaborative effort – and the recognition that there's a huge potential in developing networks, groups and communities to share good practice. She currently chairs a group of IC heads who meet monthly, bring in external speakers, create their own events, and share good practice. As she told us, somebody else will always have experienced the same challenge you're facing. Why pay £1,000 to attend a conference to get that insight when you can find it among yourselves?

The field of IC is very lucky to be populated by experienced, pragmatic and visionary characters like Shiona, who are so committed to the professionalization and advancement of their calling. We wanted to find out a little more about how this passion dovetails with the realities of IC's role in the organization now.

Annabel: Where does internal comms fit in your organization today?

Shiona: It has a seat at the top table. In my organization, it sits within the executive office, next to external communications, and the board and executive services. I have found being next to this 'dominant coalition' to be a huge advantage: knowing what's on their mind, discovering what's worrying them at first hand, being invited to make suggestions or proposals without necessarily having to prepare a paper and book a slot in the senior meeting, all makes for greater, more iterative improvement in the way the organization uses internal comms to effect change or communicate important news.

Where does it fit in terms of importance? It's becoming much more a part of the DNA. What I mean by that is the natural default position among the senior tiers is to communicate what they discuss, and communicate what they think they need people to know, all by themselves. We've set up the channels, the mechanism, the infrastructure, the advice, guidance and support for it to happen – and they are just getting on with it. The concept of 'own voice' has really been pushed forward.

IC is not a mailbox: it is an enabler. In summary, this means that we are becoming less of a deliverer of channels and much more an enabler of the story voice and systems within our organization to communicate. That is enabled by technology. It's also enabled by employee expectations, and influenced by social media trends. It's influenced as well, I think, by the increasing ability of senior managers to not have to make things perfect. The odd spelling mistake is ok, and actually makes the message all the more genuine! I laughed today when I heard a colleague say, 'If it smacks of corporate bloke – I just don't read it.'

Annabel: If you were talking to an aspiring undergraduate looking to get into IC, what would your top tips be?

Shiona: The assumption about going into IC might have been that, first and foremost, you need to be really good at writing and editing, because that's what we do. We write for channels and we edit for channels. Given all that I've said about 'own voice' and people, editing user-generated content is actually probably more important than writing from scratch. We do that too, but we also have to edit to ensure that things can be understood well. So that is a skill you need to acquire.

In light of my earlier point about the importance of data, I'd also say that understanding and upskilling yourself on research methodology is just as important as being able to write or edit well. Develop these skills early on in your career, with a focus on your ability to plan and measure.

The Government Communication Service has an excellent acronym for campaign planning called OASIS that's becoming embedded in how we approach communications more strategically and how we coach people to avoid the starting point for comms being intranet articles or posters:

Objectives

Audience/Insight

Strategy/Ideas

Implementation

Scoring/Evaluation

Set yourself some objectives around measurement – not just of the data or the different audience segments, but of the insights they deliver. That will then form a really good outcome for your communications, rather than just acting on instinct or thinking that once you've published an intranet article on the insight that's job done.

Finally, you will also need an understanding of how technology works. Don't assume, because you know how to use Snapchat or post something on Instagram, that you automatically know how Enterprise Social Networks need to work. They are massive corporate technology systems that require a combination of technology, communications and policy plus all sorts of other things to make them work well, and proper research to launch them.

Annabel: Can you expand on the value of writing and editing skills?

Shiona: Writing journalistically is good and will help people to understand what you're writing much better. To truly do the job of an internal communicator, which, in my view, is to inspire people to act differently and work towards the purpose of an organization, you need to tell a good story. It needs to set out not only the 'What we're going to do and how we're going to do it', which is the default of any corporate communication, but also the 'Why'. The 'Why' will give you the emotional elements to capture the imagination and inspire staff to act differently.

There is definitely a place for internal communicators to be great story-tellers, and to coach other people in the art of telling stories. I don't think it's something that you can just walk in and do, but if you learn how to use some descriptive narrative and use stories to make an emotional connection, you're going to inspire people to act differently. There's a whole technique and science to story-telling that I think internal communicators need to understand and equip themselves with, and coach others to use.

Compelling stories

Exploring the value of this skill was a powerful way to round off our interview. Again, we were given evidence of Shiona's commitment to the detail of the IC practitioner's role and how much it informs her decision making on a daily basis. She finished, appropriately enough, by telling us a story.

Leading into the new financial year, each of Natural England's area teams produces a document describing what they will prioritize in terms of working with partners on the ground to conserve, preserve, enhance and connect people with nature. These are usually pretty dry documents, the sort that might normally get put in a drawer. The time had come to practise what she preaches. Shiona saw an opportunity to use story-telling to create summaries of each plan: two-page documents that used lots of illustration to explain how it would benefit nature and the local economy. Working with a network of over 30 contributors, Shiona's team led a project to produce double-sided A3 documents for each of the 14 areas, which have been laminated and taken out to stakeholders, to describe and illustrate what Natural England is trying to do, at a high level, allowing people to connect what's happening in one place with opportunities and needs that might be arising elsewhere. The whole purpose was to open up a conversation about opportunities to work together in a particular place. The umbrella title of all these documents is 'It's in Our Nature'. High-quality imagery was used to illustrate the places where the organization works. Maps helped people to conceptualize what's happening. Ultimately, words turned into maps and pictures, with case studies bringing the cause and effect of activities and projects to life. Through that, a vibrant picture emerged of the diversity and beauty of the work done by Natural England.

As she drew her story to a close, Shiona observed that this entire process, rooted in best practice for IC, has made staff not only better understand, but feel more confident talking about and advocating priorities in each area. It has also opened up conversations with stakeholders in different places about new opportunities to work together. In essence, story and design turned a boring document into a dynamic tool for engagement. Perhaps the time has come for all of us to take another look at the potential of even the most unpromising collateral. It is certainly a resourceful and sustainable vision for the future of IC.

Reference

FitzPatrick, L and Valskov, K (2014) *Internal Communications: A manual for practitioners*, Kogan Page, London

Summary

We said at the beginning of this book that we would be looking at the evolution of internal communications, once a poor relation of the communications mix, into a respected discipline in its own right. In the chapters that followed, the overwhelming view shared by all those is that the IC star is on the ascendency. This ascendency is born from a whole range of business challenges that have required companies to rethink their game when communicating with staff. Sometimes driven by rapid growth or the need to engage disparate groups of people, IC is neatly positioning itself as the adhesive to facilitating an ongoing conversation – and it is about a conversation now. The broadcast era is over.

In this last chapter of *The People Business,* we wanted to devote these pages to highlights of what our interviewees have shared with us. We will present this to you as a series of themes and behaviours that will bear influence on the face of IC and, we believe, continue to shape its future.

Authentic engagement

The first theme that has found currency with many of our interviewees is that of authenticity. For Laura Ferguson at BG Group, authentic engagement comes down to how, as a senior IC leader, you assume the role of custodian of the employee experience. The employee experience, in its many forms, has required her to navigate a set of challenging interactions inside the organization with both senior and middle management. While these interactions have been ongoing, the real task has been keeping the 'heart' of the business beating with a credible narrative that employees both believe in and are empowered by.

We know from our interviewees that the need to be genuine is an overriding priority. Norman Pickavance, Grant Thornton, spoke at length about this. For him, an authentic act of kindness prevailing through the way IC works is key. At Grant Thornton, kindness is valued enormously and when a change in the business is made, a great deal of thought goes into how people will be impacted. It's unusual to hear this articulated as a natural part of the IC process in the heady world of big business, which is predominantly characterized by a time-poor, highly-driven workforce, and yet, time and investment are actively taken by the firm to ensure people are considered in the overall outcome. People are not just seen as a number on a spreadsheet but as having the ability to contribute and make the business successful.

We heard a wide range of views on what authentic engagement means in its most literal sense. Vickie Sheriff, Heathrow, believes it means 'people are aligned to what the company is doing and feel they have a voice'. The challenge for her is how you channel that voice back into the organization so it is heard and, consequently, the business can have an 'inside/out' conversation with its staff.

Norman Pickavance talked about developing this type of conversation and specifically the evolution of an unadulterated internal voice that drives essential change across the business. From a strategic viewpoint, the emphasis by his firm has been on re-inventing leaders as visionary communicators who can convey messages and strategies that are at once inspirational and realistic.

IC's role is to curate the content (sometimes referred to as 'the company narrative') and ensure the right messages land with the right people. As IC practitioners, it is a given that you have to make sure the story is relevant and resonant with everyone. One of the easiest ways to do this is by understanding your target audience and the diversity of their information needs. When the feedback is assimilated, the messages need to be tailored to different audiences along with the communications channel.

Tailoring messages to audiences within an organization is just as important as the comms channel used. Vickie Sheriff acknowledges that lengthy newsletters are things of the past. Today, the more companies grasp the power of story-telling to create engaging content that is shared internally and externally, the faster they will grow because employees will feel aligned and part of the conversation.

There are some smart road checks to get into the habit of using when trying to hone a particular point or message. For example, one essential task is to make sure the 'why we are doing this' permeates everything that is said. The more context people are given, the easier it is to grasp the reasons for a change or a move in a new direction. People feel safer when they know where they stand. Over-communicating is not advisable either and if you feel lost or out of your depth, trust your instincts and seek out colleagues to test your content.

Norman Pickavance observed how there has been a loss of tolerance for obscure and convoluted messages and how this remains a major tension for effective IC. He advocates simplicity and making the IC process as interactive as possible. Why so? It makes it much easier for people to both engage with and reflect on what they've heard. In short, messages need to be robust, stand up to internal and external scrutiny and, most important of all, be believable.

Every company featured in this book wants this authentic conversation with its employees. While each company may be at a different stage of developing that conversation, the emphasis is on taking the brave step of listening and realizing that all feedback is good feedback.

We know from our interviewees that IC can be very creative when it wants to provoke a conversation or a listening exercise and it has the luxury of a range of creative tools within arm's reach. While some businesses opt for the creative route and provide areas in the office where employees can 'break out' and be facilitated to think differently in a relaxing environment (think beanbags in the workplace), others prefer to set up easy ways for people to give regular, open and honest feedback. Whatever your preference, the essential point here is to provide the right platform or platforms to create the conversation, be part of it and listen, with broad shoulders. You have to keep listening.

Take a sensitive topic – a company merger, a situation Laura Ferguson knows well. When it comes to initiating a conversation, it is essential to support people so they understand the proper context for change because this will provide layers of psychological stability for them. Stability during any transition is in much demand. Complement this with the clear behaviours of respect, fairness, honesty and openness and you will go a long way to keeping people focused.

There is a subtlety here that is worth noting. For employees to speak their minds, they need to decide if they want to be part of the solution. A company may provide the right environment for people to develop their skills (whether that is handling a crisis or simply resolving an issue they had previously had no experience of), but how far are employees prepared to go (or drive themselves) to achieve success? This sense of collective responsibility will doubtless emerge as a prevailing theme for companies looking to behave in an open and transparent way with their employees. By doing so, there has to be a cut-off in terms of being honest and expecting that honesty to be returned.

Listening effectively

We've covered the importance of generating an authentic conversation with employees and observed that this will only be successful if the company goes out of its way to listen effectively. Time and investment are required so that staff are given a suitable way or platform to 'feed back' and share opinion. Suzanne Peck felt strongly that an essential attribute that can be easily emulated is for an IC practitioner to be endlessly curious. She sees it as a character trait that should be exploited and continually in use.

How you listen effectively is an ongoing process. There are many ways of listening and some businesses are reluctant to shake off old habits in favour of the new. In other words, companies are still relying on the annual employee engagement survey and the likelihood is they will find themselves out of date in terms of what innovative IC looks like if they do not embrace new listening techniques.

You do not need to take our word for it. We asked all of our interviewees what they thought of the annual survey in our Pulse Check™, and 67 per cent said it is dead and buried. Jenny Burns neatly summed it up with her comment, 'change is happening in business and to people personally so much, that by the time you've done the survey, got in all the responses and spent three months navigating through the results, the whole world has shifted, from a business perspective and for you individually, since that moment when you filled in the survey… I think we should be moving towards sentiment analysis and touch-points.'

Lindsey Morrell, Telefónica, agreed and asserted that the days of the annual engagement survey are numbered. Norman Pickavance also called time on it, saying it has lost fight in holding onto its original purpose. Why so? Because the fundamental question is: does an annual survey move the agenda forward and address the real issues people are talking about? In today's hyper-connected world, we would argue the annual engagement survey is an anachronism for the simple reason that the world we live in is constantly changing. We are in a state of constant flux and, as a consequence, people's views and opinions are forever placed on divert.

Our interviewees are already shunning old habits of the past and while they still see value in an annual benchmark of sorts, you cannot depend on this as your only source of feedback. A more nimble, time-sensitive approach is hailed as best practice as it allows you to keep your finger on the pulse of employee sentiment and track mood shifts in real-time. But is this enough? Not for Vickie Sheriff, who advocates that face-to-face will always be an essential component to listening successfully. Once the listening exercise is complete, the task that comes to bear down so quickly is how you are seen to be acting on the feedback.

For Jo Harvey, PizzaExpress, despite the challenges indigenous to the leisure sector in terms of retaining staff, there remains a unique opportunity to capture the 'undercurrent' of sentiment in terms of why people leave the restaurant business. In short, finding out what's working and what's not when a member of staff leaves is gold dust to a time-poor and highly competitive business. Building trends from the data that capture the regional perspective gives a business such as PizzaExpress a head start in the recruitment process and the opportunity to course-correct the employee experience along the way.

Other people leaving the organization will share the greatest truth, and one significant investment PizzaExpress has made is to track that conversation and analyse the feedback. In other words, the company is listening and gathering brilliant ideas for how to improve. The learning here must surely be to keep listening broadly and deeply. Every piece of feedback is an investment in your business, no matter what sector you are in and no matter how bad it is.

The 'arrive with data, leave with respect' mantra quoted by Shiona Adamson (FitzPatrick and Valskov, 2014) chimes with her belief that data complements the ear to the ground gut feel. Managing feedback and listening to employees is a science rather than just acting on assumptions. As companies continue to measure and track how effective IC boosts productivity and business delivery, it won't be long before we are equation-rich in terms of what good looks like.

All of our interviewees recognized the listening exercise as the cornerstone of any successful IC strategy. Identifying the tiers of management that can block effective listening and taking action helps. Middle managers can sometimes be the gatekeepers to making IC work well. Training is a prerequisite to ensure these managers feel confident and equipped to both share the feedback and explain the company's plan to take positive action.

Suzanne Peck asserts that line managers are the lynchpin in driving behaviour change following any employee feedback. This is backed up by our other interviewees. Involving this tier of management should remain a priority for any IC campaign or launch in progress. Simply put, middle management is where change happens. It's what the everyday employee sees and hears. It is the coalface of internal communications working at its best.

Ultimately, it is a team game. For a company to listen and an employee, in return, to assess his or her abilities and identify where he or she needs support or more opportunity, is an active dialogue. It is a dialogue built on trust that if help is asked for, it will be given and the individual will be supported. Consequently, high flyers need to know the company they work for is committed to giving them every chance to succeed and spread their wings.

The listening exercise has to be all-embracing. A regular topic with our interviewees was the impact that millennials are having in the workplace. It is a given that they are motivated by values and genuinely want to be part of the conversation. They are not interested in the 'broadcast' approach. They need to feel involved. They want to have a voice.

It's intriguing to delve a little further to understand what's driving this. In Vickie Sheriff's mind, much of this comes down to how much millennials have personally invested in their education. They, as a consequence, want a tangible ROI and to be trusted, involved and have responsibility. They are especially sensitive to any sniff of corporate whitewash. In fact, any suggestion of 'over-messaged' content coming their way and millennials will disengage with considerable speed.

Suzanne Peck, IoIC and The Sequel Group, pointed out that it's important to remember that 80 per cent of organizations are multi-generational so we should not play hostage to the rise of the millennials in the workplace. They are still a part of the internal voice but are yet to dominate it. There are easy ways to make relationships work internally by buddying up older staff with younger talent so that they can learn from each other.

When buddying doesn't work, try a little coaching, as advocated by Helen den Held, GE Capital. Her story was representative of many companies today in terms of doing all the basics well and, at the same time, making their way towards new employee engagement tools and methodologies. These methodologies include coaching and have given Helen time to explore new techniques to improve communication dynamics. Inside GE Capital, she has set her stall around effective coaching as a way to generate trust and employee interaction. It's resonating particularly well with the millennials in her team. So much so that these coaching skills are now used as a core element of her IC strategy and are actively supporting an ongoing dialogue with the management team. She welcomes transparency at all levels and, along with it, the need to involve employees in the constant development of the company narrative.

A valuable litmus test Laura Ferguson shared is how effective the directors and CEO end up being as a result of employee opinion. Employee expectation today is demanding they become more involved, with the key measure being how quickly they act on the feedback with their teams. There are management techniques available to help the IC practitioner handle these types of sensitive situations carefully and achieve the right result for the business as well as for the individuals concerned. Yet how can you tell a senior leader he or she needs to be more involved and not upset them in the process? One of those techniques is knowing how to challenge respectfully. While this is a skill that requires a significant amount of emotional intelligence, when done well it can help build respect and trust. For some, it's a case of having an open conversation and being very clear that that is what it is. For others, it requires time and a lot of coaching to gently coax out what really lies beneath.

This brings us neatly to looking at the captain of the narrative. It is essential that every business has a clear purpose and this has to be well articulated by the CEO. If there is a resting point for our book, it must surely be with the role the CEO plays in IC. In a recent Pulse Check™, we asked our IC community for their views on how well their CEO communicates with his or her staff. We asked four questions, shown in Figure S.1:

1 Is your CEO a natural when it comes to internal communications?

2 When communicating internally, how authentic and compelling is your CEO's voice?

3 How good is your CEO at communicating across the generations of staff you have eg, X, Y, Z, etc?

4 If there is one thing your CEO is brilliant at, what is it?

Each gave excellent insight into how CEOs are grappling with the need to have a more 'public' role inside the company they work for. Some do this well by walking the floor or simply working unscripted in front of groups of staff. Others find it hard to bridge the gap between communicating with their leadership team (which feels natural to them) and their frontline staff where the authenticity of what they say is under the microscope. Some of our respondents observed that CEOs do well when they make a personal connection with the people they are addressing and those that are quick to grasp the new norms of working practice thrive in their public role.

The results paint a clear picture that there is a balance to be struck between ability and delivery. What we mean by that is that some CEOs may find it easy to communicate, feel they were born for it, but have to match that ability with sensitive delivery. Giving a straight answer to a straight question is essential. Also, feeling comfortable

Figure S.1 CEO communication Pulse Check™

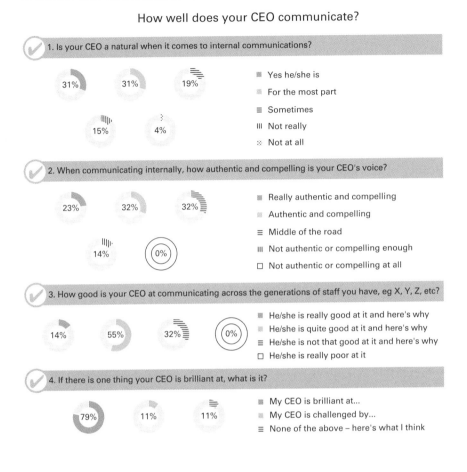

How well does your CEO communicate?

1. Is your CEO a natural when it comes to internal communications?

31% 31% 19%

15% 4%

- Yes he/she is
- For the most part
- Sometimes
- Not really
- Not at all

2. When communicating internally, how authentic and compelling is your CEO's voice?

23% 32% 32%

14% 0%

- Really authentic and compelling
- Authentic and compelling
- Middle of the road
- Not authentic or compelling enough
- Not authentic or compelling at all

3. How good is your CEO at communicating across the generations of staff you have, eg X, Y, Z, etc?

14% 55% 32% 0%

- He/she is really good at it and here's why
- He/she is quite good at it and here's why
- He/she is not that good at it and here's why
- He/she is really poor at it

4. If there is one thing your CEO is brilliant at, what is it?

79% 11% 11%

- My CEO is brilliant at...
- My CEO is challenged by...
- None of the above – here's what I think

Date: 30/11/2016

with a tough love approach, ie communicating the hard messages, will invoke more positive reactions. Employees are always smarter than we think and can see through the corporate-speak very quickly. A CEO who speaks from the heart and is open and realistic will earn more respect than one who shies away from telling it how it is. Authenticity is the name of the game.

Managing change

Change is a theme that Laura Ferguson knows intimately. The topic of change is not unusual, particularly in multinational businesses. In our discussion, we examined how the employer brand can become a dynamic and innovative power tool to unite the workforce throughout corporate change. Yet before arriving at the definition of an 'employer brand', you need to understand what this brand stands for and you can only do this by developing a broader understanding of the business. The beauty of working with or talking to other functions in the business is that you acquire a real sense of what it's like to work for the company.

Experience is a great teacher; Laura talked about the things you shouldn't do when working in a transformational environment. One of them is the pitfall of creating the cult of a leader. Too much aggrandizing can end up isolating people from the company's wider purpose and the danger then of becoming disaffected.

Jenny Burns, Just, described how IC comes into its own at a time of crisis, always a happy bed partner to change. Every company has to face issues or situations that require 'positive' management and this is when IC can show its value. Perhaps, when a company is in the middle of making a part of its workforce redundant, it is unthinkable that it could boost productivity, but here is a suggestion to consider. If a company focuses on honesty and integrity in communicating difficult news in times of change, there is a strong possibility that people remain engaged because they feel involved and they know what's going on.

While all this change in IC is going on around us, there are some companies that are preoccupied with the all-important task of running a commercially successful business. Jo Harvey and Suzie Welch, PizzaExpress, presented a different face of IC within their organization where financial performance takes precedence at every level. Very much seen as a luxury discipline, IC has to fight hard to position itself alongside the operational focus of the business. Often, the challenge of running a highly competitive business is that the operational demands will outweigh the people priorities. Also, in a business that has been managing change for over 50 years, these dynamics are unlikely to change. So the question is, how do you work with the lot you've been given?

According to Jo Harvey, the overriding goal has to be to keep painting the emotional picture of how people are feeling up the chain. Sometimes extended and excessive repetition can prove itself a mighty attention seeker and be heard despite being in an environment where the topic of financial performance presides. Whatever the reasons or catalysts for commercial success, at some point senior management want to know what's driving growth and what's not. It's the 'what's not' that commands the lion's share of attention and that is when IC can elbow its way into the discussion and offer the internal view. As Jo Harvey will attest, many of the answers lie with the employee base.

Equally, Suzanne Peck has watched and participated in the sea change of IC evolving from a back office function to a mainstream, credible and active communications discipline. She spoke of the duality of managing an engaged workforce alongside the pressures of business to deliver superior financial performance. While we can wistfully position IC as the communications discipline that ties the whole business together, the reality is that every company needs to make money to survive.

How can IC practitioners take advantage of this or at least move the business agenda on? For some companies today, the idea of grasping the nettle and accepting that what some may still see as 'fluffy stuff' is an IC alchemist's delight because a boost in productivity will deliver a positive financial return. We all know this to be true. The exciting part of this equation is to look for new ways to expand a company and deliver that positive return.

The best place to start, says Suzanne Peck, is to be curious about the business you are in. Getting under the skin of what your company does, how challenging some of its operations can be and how it makes money will shine a light on the commercial realities and how hard success can be to attain. From here, you can build an action path for IC to champion the successes and tackle the challenges inside and out. The goal of course is making the employees part of the journey.

The future of IC

Now that we are at the end of our book, we wanted to bring together all the collective observations and lessons and present these to you as a set of reminders as to what the future might look like in all things IC.

Lindsey Morrell believes there is a clear opportunity for IC to take advantage of some of the new digital tools on offer that can help capture the interest and attention of the new generations in a time-sensitive way. People have short attention spans and want their information to come quickly and be easily understood – and the more visual the better. We all know that e-mail is no longer the best tool for communicating change or news.

For many organizations, the challenge is how to overcome the mismatch between the need to communicate, and the IT infrastructure in place. A lot of companies are still 'revolutionizing' and shaking off the shackles of old-fashioned communications tools while grasping the nettle of managing 'Big Data'. With Big Data come added responsibilities and an increasing level of scrutiny in terms of how personal information is held and shared. Couple this with the increasingly blurred boundaries between external and internal communications and you have a whole other set of considerations.

Our recommendation is to start small. A fledgling project, if successful, will work its magic around the organization for the simple reason that good gets noticed. Also remember, that while technology has an important part to play, the value of face-to-face is the die-hard feedback mechanism of choice.

The future will be about creating channels that empower employees to communicate how and when they want. This is an attractive proposition. In a world where the expectation of transparency is becoming the norm, the more people are encouraged to speak openly and thrive on a 'community-led' approach in terms of having their issues resolved, the more trust will be built between company and stakeholder. Everyone feels relief when a problem is overcome. By resolving the smaller issues on a daily basis, employees feel more empowered and engaged.

An organization can only ever be as good as the people who work for it, attested Fiona Shepherd. It's a truth that applies to any kind of company. Whatever you provide for your clients, it always comes back to the people who build and develop products or services, who grow your market, who engage your customers and forge relationships. Without them, you don't have a business.

The face of IC is changing. There has been a sea change in how IC is perceived by teams and leaders. It is now a cross-team, cross-function discipline. IC also has clear targets. It is there to engage people in not just the company story, but the business strategy, objectives, purpose, goals and vision. IC is no longer about broadcasting messages. In fact, as a communication discipline, it is on the cusp of some extraordinary opportunities for innovation. That innovation may come from unexpected places but it will be disruptive and driven by the wider environment we live in. The age of the blue-collar worker is on the wane. We are all stakeholders in the companies we work for. We all have a voice and all of them count.

Conclusion

At the time of writing this chapter, Europe and the United States have borne witness to two, unprecedented political events. The first was the 52 per cent vote in favour of Brexit by the British population. The second was the decision by 60-odd million Americans to vote in the first US President with no political office experience.

Prior to the EU referendum and the US election, pollsters had it in the bag for the opposition. Even though each event was likely to be close to call, the prevailing view was that Brits would want to stay in the comfortable, bureaucracy-rich environs of the EU. Equally, most believed that Hillary Clinton would become the first female US President. Neither happened. So while every political analyst spent the subsequent days and weeks racking his or her political brains as to why the protagonist prevailed on each occasion, it is perhaps the views of the silent majority that offer some insight. Some observers maintain that Trump won because he was saying what everyone was thinking. Constantly. He eschewed caution and every time he had his knuckles wrapped for going too far, he extended his rhetoric and kept going. He left his opponent high and dry. Whether the climate for change was with him or not, there was clearly something in his diktat that appealed. And yet, this wasn't picked up in the polls.

Much time has been spent on what drove people to vote for Trump given his outlandish statements and prolific, provocative presence on social media. Clinton has since publicly blamed the FBI for her defeat (see http://www.nytimes.com/2016/11/13/us/politics/hillary-clinton-james-comey.html?_r=0), but the sentiment that drove Trump to unexpected success is still being explored. Did he win because people simply will say one thing and then do another? Or is it that people find it hard to articulate their truth when they know it is (possibly) the wrong thing to think in today's progressive, politically correct society? Is it all too easy for a presidential candidate to enter stage left and speak openly about real people's fears and concerns and by doing so, legitimize them?

The analysis continues as we write this but we wonder if it is possible to draw parallels here to what really goes on inside businesses today. Are employees paying lip service to the corporate vision when in fact, inside, they are yearning to work for a company that really 'gets' the world they live in? Do they long for a work culture that understands how expensive it is to buy a house; how much a pint costs in a London pub as opposed to in a country village; having children and paying for childcare leaves little or no 'fun' money for a couple let alone a single parent? Are employees ever asked if they are happy within themselves, with their lot? Generally not. In our discussions, the 'happiness' factor did not come up as a consideration. If it did, happiness was aligned to satisfaction with job lot and role within the organization. That's not to say our interviewees didn't believe that personal happiness was important. It is more that the purpose of IC remains driven by the bigger business agenda.

Businesses realize there is tangible advantage to having their workforce engaged. In the absence of employee productivity equations, it doesn't take a rocket scientist to work out that if you're engaged and enjoying a task, you are likely to do it well. The reality is that the majority of IC-led surveys or discussions focus on what will make the business better and how to improve the way we work, optimize productivity, in short, make more money. There's nothing wrong with this of course. Employees want to be asked what they think and they want their working environment to be inspiring and to be part of a great company. They want to self-actualize.

Recently, the external debate to have employees become an active part of the board is driving news headlines in the United Kingdom (thanks to the BHS fallout earlier in 2016 and Prime Minister Theresa May's subsequent decision to champion the worker; see https://www.ft.com/content/d7ba161e-2423-11e6-9d4d-c11776a5124d and https://www.politicshome.com/news/uk/economy/taxation/news/80965/full-text-theresa-mays-speech-cbi for more on these issues). Whatever the outcome, even if the government decides to play down its declaration to give the employee a greater voice, the fact remains that businesses today have to pay more attention. For some, this will mean rethinking their entire game when it comes to initiating a positive conversation with their workforce.

Perhaps there is a perfect opportunity here for IC to create its own authentic role by making the lives of the people it speaks for better: doing a better job of understanding the happiness factor among staff, in particular what inspires them and whether they are listened to as this will go a long way to making them feel valued. Recognizing and bringing awareness to mental health and wellbeing in the workplace is something we have not touched on in this book but is an area that needs more attention.

It is several steps forward from the CSR-led programmes we see some companies running. These give staff a day off to work for a charity or collect litter in their local neighbourhood in an effort to recognize that the act of giving can release huge amounts of personal satisfaction. Norman Pickavance touched on it in his interview. As we mentioned earlier, he spoke of the role of kindness (in the context of having an authentic conversation), the ability of managers and senior leaders to take some time to share and empathize on, for example, the reality of being a working parent, etc. It's those little touches or moments to stop and just talk that make people feel they are part of a company that really does genuinely care about them. No longer a number in the P&L or the charmingly termed 'headcount' but an individual with a rocket full of skills and ambition, just waiting to take off.

This book has devoted a lot of its pages to the art of conversation. We have looked at how companies are increasingly keen to unlock honest, open discussions with their staff and not penalize people for telling their truth. Could it be, though, that in light of this conversation, there is an opening for a new approach to IC that embraces the 'whole' employee and talks their kind of language? For all surveys that can be done, all the focus groups that can be run, all the town halls that can be held, do people leave the room each time, cursing themselves for failing to speak their truth? Are companies today still failing to provide the right environment to help people say what they think, hear that truth and react positively?

How many of us come to work and play a part? How many of us leave work and become our real selves? Unlocking our inner selves in the workplace is an intriguing concept because most people are expected to turn up with the singular goal of doing their job and going home. Even if some are hypnotized by what they do and how it contributes to the greater good (for that read 'greater profit'), there must surely be a point at which the worker meets the human and the two interact. It's food for thought.

We have learnt in this book that everyone's opinion counts. Everyone wants and deserves to be heard. If we all connected together more and by doing so linked different groups of people together, we might just reach a point where we all know what is actually going on. It takes courage, it takes patience, a willingness to listen and, most important of all, several leaps of faith.

Reference

FitzPatrick, L and Valskov, K (2014) *Internal Communications: A manual for practitioners*, Kogan Page, London

TWENTY TOP TIPS FOR SUCCESSFUL INTERNAL COMMUNICATORS

1 Embrace variety, be open, outgoing and honest.

2 Network, be interested in people.

3 Develop good listening skills.

4 Know your audience and stakeholders.

5 Adopt a continuous improvement mindset.

6 Be accepting of constructive criticism.

7 Develop a thick skin and be prepared for things to not always go quite to plan.

8 Decide what you want to be famous for and ensure you have the core skills to deliver and achieve it.

9 Be bold in your level of communications and consistent with your messaging.

10 Understand how technology works, eg social media.

11 Appreciate how busy managers are.

12 Live, eat and breathe the culture you live in.

13 Look for opportunities to create a genuinely connected conversation across your business.

14 Work for an organization that is closely aligned to your personal values and aspirations.

15 Don't forget about the balance of health and family alongside your work.

16 Don't worry about having lots of direct contact with the CEO/senior leaders to begin with.

17 Don't try to control everything.

18 Practise what you preach.

19 Become a natural curator of content.

20 Always work hard and with passion – or don't do it at all.

INDEX

Note: The index is filed in alphabetical, word-by-word order. Within main headings, numbers are filed as spelt out in full and acronyms filed as presented. Page locators in *italics* denote information contained within a Figure or Table.